THE ART OF SINGLE LIVING

A Guide to Going
It Alone in the '90s

THE ART OF SINGLE LIVING

A Guide to Going It Alone in the '90s

RUTHE STEIN

Nationally Syndicated Columnist

SHAPOLSKY PUBLISHERS, INC.
NEW YORK

A Shapolsky Book

For any additional information, contact:
Shapolsky Publishers, Inc.
136 West 22nd Street, NY, NY 10011
(212) 633-2022

10 9 8 7 6 5 4 3 2 1

I S B N 1 - 5 6 1 7 1 - 0 0 1 - 6

Typeset by Printworks Limited, Madison, CT

Printed and bound by Graficromo s.a., Córdoba, Spain

To the memory of my parents, Lillian and Jack Begun.
And to Dean, and the future.

CONTENTS

CONTENTS

Acknowledgments

I would like to thank Iris Frost, editor of the "People" section at the *San Francisco Chronicle*, for coming up with the idea for a "singles" column and entrusting it to me. Thanks are also due to all the others at the newspaper who supported my work, especially William German, executive editor, Rosalie Muller Wright, assistant managing editor, and Phelps Dewey, assistant to the publisher. I am indebted to Stuart Dodds, general manager of Chronicle Features, for recognizing the potential for a wider market for the column and for all his efforts to syndicate it. Grateful acknowledgment is made to the *San Francisco Chronicle* for permission to reprint these columns.

For their judicious editing and clever headlines, thanks go to Jean Arnold, Stan Arnold, Craig Black, Connie Ballard, Deborah Bergman, Andrea Behr, Marybeth Bizjak, Mark Lundgren and Lynda MacNamara. Thanks go also to Dorine Iacone and Mike Keiser for their computer expertise and to Linda Avery for her assistance when I needed it. And special thanks are due Michael Robertson for never being too busy to help me choose between two words and for always knowing which was the better one.

I am grateful to my friends—too numerous to list—who gave me ideas and support, and to the thousands of readers who have written to me over the years. Their encouragement keeps me going.

Ruthe Stein
San Francisco
1990

ix

HOW I GOT SO SMART:
A PERSONAL INTRODUCTION

With the thousands of letters readers have sent me, I'm still waiting for one that asks the question I have asked myself: What qualifies you to tell single people how to lead their lives?

Working for a newspaper imbues you with an instant expertise. I learned this when I was just starting in the business and was assigned to answer the fashion editor's phone. I suddenly became the voice of authority on how to dress. My favorite fashion question was: "What should I wear to an affair?" Though I knew that callers meant a wedding or bar mitzvah, not an assignation, I was still tempted to reply, "As little as possible."

Now my name above a column has turned me into an

authority on singles. My readers appear to have accepted me as such and, after a great deal of soul searching, I've determined that their trust has not been misplaced. I do know what I'm talking about when I talk about being single. Everything I know I've learned from experience; it really is the best teacher. Of most consequence, I have learned to be happy on my own. The older I get, the more I realize happiness is what it's all about. Yet so many people, who appear to have everything going for them, make themselves unhappy worrying that they'll never marry instead of appreciating all that single life has to offer.

I haven't always been this smart. I was born in 1945, which makes me part of the last generation of women to be raised with the belief that there would always be a man to take care of us. Talk about dumb beliefs to grow up with!

Fortunately, my mother also believed I should be able to support myself just in case, so, when I finished college, I had acquired not just a husband, but also a career. I went directly from the family home to a sorority house to being *at home* with my husband, as our wedding announcement quaintly put it. I had a very traditional marriage in which my husband did all the things men are supposed to do and I performed all the wifely chores.

I never lived alone until I was thirty-three and newly divorced. One of my sorority sisters was Sherry Lansing, who went on to be the first woman president of a Hollywood studio. She had also married right out of school, but she split from her husband a few years later. I sometimes wonder what heights I might have reached if I hadn't waited twelve years to get a divorce.

However, at first I was terrified to be on my own. It became a point of pride not to show it. With each new task I would master, whether it was hanging pictures on the wall with no assistance or being able to spend an entire evening alone in my apartment without freaking out, I would be like the hoofer in *A Chorus Line* who silently proclaimed, "I can do that."

When you haven't been single for a long time, you think nobody will ask you out and that you will go home every night to the Great Books. But men did ask me out. And I asked a few of them out. It seemed the less I needed a man, the easier it was to find one.

Part of the art of single living is to act confident even when you don't feel it, and to know you are just as all right at home alone on a Saturday night as out on a date. There are a lot of potential students who need to master this art. The number of singles in their thirties doubled in the 1980s; by the end of this decade, it has been predicted that half the population will be single.

I'm delighted to be able to pass on what I have learned.

PARTY OF ONE

Everybody has been single. Some of us marry and then become single again. We may even repeat this cycle a few times. A growing number of people, either by intention or circumstance, will never marry.

Whether being single is a stage you're going through or your permanent destination, you need to know the basics, such as how to make a comfortable home for one—a place where you will want to live, not just sleep—and how to manage your financial affairs. The dividends from these are more long term than from affairs of the heart.

Singles should also learn to keep themselves entertained— which may mean doing things alone when there's no one to do them with. In times of trouble, you may wish you had a hand to hold. But there's some consolation in knowing you'll come through fine on your own.

For a Good Time, Ask Yourself Out

When I returned from three months in Europe, I found people weren't curious about the things I had done, but that I had done them alone. They couldn't believe I had ordered dinner for one at the three-star restaurants of Paris, attended theater in London every night by myself and wandered unaccompanied through Hamburg's bawdy St. Pauli district. For my ventures, I was called "courageous"—the same woman who never learned to ski because she was too terrified to get up the mountain.

I guess because I have been going places by myself since I was a kid, I never thought it was an unnatural state. The world, after all, is not Noah's Ark: You don't have to travel in pairs to be allowed in. However, many people would apparently rather stay cloistered in their rooms than be seen without an escort after dark. They seem to think they will be stared at and branded as friendless and unlovable. Not true. People are usually too absorbed in their own conversation to notice if you came in alone or with an orangutan.

There are actually many advantages to being by yourself. You don't have to apologize when the restaurant of your choice burns the entrée. You'll always win the argument about which movie to see. You can usually wrangle a ticket to a sold-out concert. You'll also be more approachable and therefore have a better chance of meeting next week's date.

But I have no illusions about convincing anyone that it's better to be alone. I'm just saying to singles who complain about missing things because of not having anyone to go with: Go by yourself.

Probably the easiest place to start is the movies. It's a solitary activity anyway and so dark inside that nobody will see you. Just be sure you have a jacket to leave behind when you go for popcorn. Remember, you won't have anybody to save your seat. Live entertainment is more of a challenge. There are sure to be couples milling around, so be prepared to feel that everybody has somebody to talk to except you. You could spend intermission at your seat feeling sorry for yourself, but what I would do—in fact, what I *do* do—is adopt a superior attitude. Stroll through the lobby as if it were your living room and observe what your "guests" are wearing.

To pull off that kind of detached arrogance, you'll need to look absolutely smashing yourself. Don't make the mistake of thinking you can wear any old thing when you're out alone. With everything else you're going to be self-conscious about, you should at least feel confident about your appearance.

I know some people can't enjoy a performance or even a ball game unless they have someone to share it with. However, I've found it's easier to concentrate when you're not worrying about whether your companion likes the show—or whether he or she likes you. And if you don't like the show, you can just walk out. No explanations necessary.

O.K., now for the really tough one. How about dining alone— and I don't mean at the local hot dog stand. I suggest starting with an empty restaurant: On a Monday night, you can have your pick of them. The waiters will be far more uneasy than you are. They'll flurry around your table like you're royalty. The bad time will be between courses, when it's just you and an empty plate. Bring a book to read if you must, but better yet, find a restaurant that has music.

When you're ready, also find one that has people. Undistracted by a dinner partner, it's easier to eavesdrop on other people's conversations. Those between husbands and wives always make me grateful to be alone.

You'll be fine once your food arrives. But do try to control the tendency of many solitary diners to eat too fast. You might count to ten between bites or try to figure out if the hair on the aging

11

gentleman next to you is really his.

How you are treated will depend a lot on your behavior. Never apologize for being alone or make excuses. The maître d' does not need to know that your date stood you up. When asked how many in your party, don't say, "Just one." Do couples say, "Just two?" You have the same rights as the other diners. If you feel you were passed over for a table because you're alone, or that your waiter is ignoring you, don't cower. Complain to the management.

When you can handle all of the above, you're ready to travel solo. Again, the important thing is your attitude. Think of it as embarking on an adventure—not being exiled to Siberia. Do everything you can to assure that you won't be lonely. Arrange a trip to the Mardi Gras or some kind of arts festival where there will be lots going on. Plan activities to keep you busy from morning till night; the morning ones are important to get you out of your hotel room early. Take trains and buses rather than driving by yourself, which is too isolating. (Of course, you could always take a tour, but don't ask me about that. I hate tours.)

Ask friends if they know anyone in the places where you will be, and don't be shy about calling them. I've found people are more likely to offer to show you around or invite you over if you're on your own.

For your first few outings, I would advise against countries where you don't speak the language, especially if you're a talker like me. It's frustrating not to be able to chat with the natives—particularly when you may have no one else to talk to.

When you long to hear a familiar voice, it's fine to call your friends back home. Just make it brief and save the details for your return. You might also think about keeping a journal of your trip, including your thoughts on being alone. Or tell it to a tape recorder. It's a way of legitimately talking to yourself.

Singles Can't Depend on Others to Entertain Them

Getting married is more than an emotional commitment; it's a commitment of time. The full promise is to love, honor, obey and hang out together.

Single people have the same number of hours to fill, but with no one around to help fill them. No one is telling you to be home at a certain hour. The hard truth is that no one cares if you come home at all. You are totally responsible for planning your own time. However, there is no blueprint for how to do it. The experts have jumped in to give people advice on combining a career with a family. But how do you combine a career with a void?

What too often happens is that work gobbles up all your waking hours. It is something to do, a place to feel needed. Political candidates have learned that unattached people make the best campaign managers. They will stick it out on the hustings long after the rest of the staff has retreated.

Another mistake singles make is to emulate the way couples spend their free time. Since they tend to stay home, the peculiar notion has developed that's where *everybody* should be. I know too many people who rent a half-dozen movies on Friday night and spend the weekend alone with their VCR. That seems an unfortunate, if unintentional, way in which technology is being used to isolate those who are already isolated.

By contrast, in the last century you would have passed the time with family members, accompanying them from parlor to parlor for a game of whist or charades. The maiden aunt and bachelor uncle were staples of nineteenth-century literature, lovingly written about by, among others, Jane Austen, herself a spinster. But in this day and age, especially in California, singles live like waifs disconnected from their families and past. As a result, friendships have become more important than ever. There's a danger, though, of becoming too dependent on your

13

friends—expecting them to be combination surrogate spouses and siblings.

So what is a single person to do? If you're feeling as if you have too much time on your hands, you might consider these suggestions, all of which work for me:

• Get out of the house. It helps if, like me, you have the mentality of an activities director on a cruise ship. Once you start looking, you'll find there are endless things to do and that some of them, such as concerts in the park and street fairs, are even free.

• Invite people over. Singles, especially the male of the species, seem to feel that entertaining is the exclusive domain of couples. To see how easy it can be, the next time you're going to be home watching whichever sport is in season, ask a few of your buddies to bring some beer and come on over.

• Hang out. I prefer to do this at the kind of cafe where I can sit for hours without the owner demanding the table back. If you don't go there to get picked up, bars are another good place to just sort of be. The British have been hanging out at them for centuries.

• Do something physical. Choose a type of exercise like bicycling, running or long-distance walking that will allow you to explore the area where you live—while you're getting healthy.

• Do something intellectual. Whether it's taking a class, attending a lecture about a new museum show or reading the Great Books, it will make you feel good, if not smug. You have the time to learn new things. Why not use it?

• Finally, start to rely on yourself. It's unreasonable to expect other people to entertain you. The hardest part about being single is coming face to face with yourself.

A Matter of Age, Style

When my aunt Thelma lost her husband fifteen years ago, she packed her belongings, including the sectional with the gold slipcovers, and moved to Miami Beach. The family worried about how she would adjust to living alone, just as they worried about me after my divorce. From what I could tell, talking to my eighty-year-old aunt on that sectional for many hours, she has managed just fine.

Because of our ages and temperaments, we have adapted differently. The important thing, though, is that we both have adapted.

Aunt Thelma and "the girls"—as she refers to her women friends, most of whom are about her age—get together regularly to play cards and Mah-Jongg or to wander around the shopping malls. When my aunt isn't with "the girls," she comes up with projects to keep herself busy. She seems forever to be baking cookies or pasting photos of her grandchildren and great-grand-children into albums. My aunt, who never lived alone until she was sixty-five, has found, to her surprise, that she enjoys it. She stays up as late as she feels like watching TV. Her condo is in meticulous order. We laughed about how nice it is not to have someone else move things from where we put them.

She is content enough with her life to have no desire to remarry. She has had several opportunities, she wanted me to know, and has run away from all of them. The way my aunt sees it, if a man her age has money and his health, he is interested in women twenty or thirty years younger. Any eighty-year-old who would ask her to marry him basically wants someone to take care of him—and why would she want to do that?

Yet for all her feistiness and independence, there are all sorts of things my aunt won't do. She won't go anywhere by herself, not even to the corner deli, where she could sit at the counter. Although she used to love parties, she hasn't attended any of those in her building. It would be different if she had a husband to escort her, she says.

She has the belief common to her generation that a woman is not quite complete without a man. She worries about what people will think seeing her alone, and there was nothing I could say to convince her that most likely they wouldn't think anything.

I took her to a fancy restaurant one night. We arrived fifteen

15

minutes early and, though there were empty tables, the maître d' asked us to wait. "This would never happen if we were with a man," my aunt whispered to me. "Women just aren't treated as well when they're by themselves." I told her that that hasn't been my experience and that I sometimes seem to get better service. Aunt Thelma didn't believe me—not even when, at the precise time of our reservation, we were ushered to the best table in the house.

I think nothing of going to a restaurant or anywhere else alone, but I am incapable of staying home the way my aunt does. I wouldn't know what to do with myself. She sees her apartment as a haven; I see mine as a place to sleep. She makes real meals for herself, not the cheese and crackers her niece dines on. My aunt will cook a chicken and have it for four nights. I can't plan ahead twenty-four hours.

We are both single by choice, though that is probably not how she would describe herself. I understand why she hasn't remarried. I'm not at all sure she understands why I haven't. Though my aunt hardly ever questions me about my personal life lest she appear to be prying, late one night, she did ask if I had a boyfriend. "Yes," I told her, "I do—and a very nice one at that."

She looked visibly relieved. "Oh, good," she said. "Maybe some day when I was tired of living alone, I would marry him and settle down." I smiled. There didn't seem much point doing anything else.

Gimme Shelter—but Keep It Simple

The woman next to me was in ecstasy over the striped-silk taffeta drapes at the decorator showhouse, while her friend simply had to know how the walls had been made to look antique and if it could be done to her walls. All I wanted to know was a way out of there so I wouldn't have to look at fifteen more rooms with the latest in draped windows and *faux* wall treatments.

I had come because I used to enjoy wandering through showhouses. I would marvel at how clever the decorators were at mixing colors and patterns and finding the perfect accessories to tie a room together.

During my married life, which is beginning to feel like one of those previous incarnations Shirley MacLaine talks about, I actually had a decorator do a house for me. He was so clever, it wound up splashed all over *Architectural Digest*. (In the article, I was called a "professional writer," presumably because it sounded more important than a mere writer.)

As proud as I was of that house, I didn't want anything to do with it after I was divorced. It was too big and too much responsibility. I wasn't sure whether I could take care of myself, let alone a three-story building. Besides, the house had memories. I needed to move somewhere with a future, not a past.

I settled into a cozy five-room condominium, which I decorated myself in a style I think of as Single Person Functional. For instance, there is one good reading lamp in the living room and one chair that hogs the entire bay view. My place probably wouldn't impress *Architectural Digest*, but it suits me fine. I especially like looking at all the things I have brought back from trips.

I have given no thought to redecorating, and based on my quick exit from the decorator showhouse, if I did think of it, it would probably be with horror. I just can't make myself care about that stuff anymore.

While I don't mean to set up the way I live as a paragon of single living, it has a lot to recommend it. I believe you should make a home for yourself and not put that on hold until you get married. You could be holding for a very long time.

Of course, being single is no reason to live like a graduate student in a studio apartment with cinder-block bookcases and a single bed that doubles as a couch. By all means, surround yourself with some space, real furniture and objects that mean something to you. On the other hand, I worry about singles emulating couples and taking this home business too seriously. I don't know whether you really should be reading shelter

17

magazines for decorating tips or covering everything in chintz or purchasing state-of-the-art video equipment.

If you make your nest too comfortable, you may be tempted not to leave it, and then you'll never meet anyone. Nobody is going to knock on your door and say, "I understand there's an interesting person in there."

Isolation is always a problem for singles. You could be making it worse by settling into a house by yourself, especially if it means moving to the suburbs because that's where you can afford to buy. In some ways, an apartment or condo makes more sense than a house if you live alone. However, I'm opposed to those apartment complexes exclusively for singles—which seem to me another form of isolation. I share a building with eleven other people. We're all busy and hardly ever run into each other; still, it's reassuring to know they are there.

My upstairs neighbor watches my place when I'm away. She also watches out for me. Knowing that I almost always do something after work, when she heard me home one evening, she called to make sure I was O.K. I wonder whether she realizes how comforted I was by her concern.

Where you live, as well as what you do with that space, raises the larger issue of how you want to live as a single.

I choose to do most of my living outside of the home. That's why I have kept my actual living space simple. Since I'm not tied down to a husband, why should I be tied down to a big house or a garden—or care what's showing at the decorator showhouse?

Doing Things My Way

As I returned the oregano to its rightful place on my spice rack between the nutmeg and the paprika and lined up the bottles of Calistoga one behind the other in the refrigerator and the sticks of butter alongside each other in a straight row, it occurred to me that I would not be an easy person to live with. The ways in which I have become "set" make perfect sense to me. But what would someone make of them who didn't see the logic of alphabetizing your spices and record albums and arranging your wardrobe by color and fabric and your books by height?

It doesn't strike me as odd to fluff up the cushions on my couch the instant I get up. But would that habit seem peculiar to another person if it were his imprint continually being erased?

After a dinner party, I can't rest until my apartment has been put back to pristine condition. I am like that fairy-tale princess kept awake by an errant pea. But had there been a prince sharing her bed, would he have put up with her nocturnal tossing and turning? Similarly, a bachelor I know who piles bills on top of the stove might not be considered a good catch by a woman who is a gourmet cook.

As long as there's no hubby stockpiling food, it's just fine that my friend Mary keeps her cookbooks in the refrigerator and that my friend Patti stores her pantyhose in the freezer. Someone once told her it makes them last longer. Yes, in answer to your next question, she defrosts them before wearing.

If nobody is looking for the salt shaker, it doesn't matter that Ken has made a permanent home for it on the TV stand. And with no pleas for silence, Jack has gone ahead and put speakers in every room in his house, including the bathroom.

When you live alone you can get away with washing your clothes by stomping on them while you're in the shower, throwing stuff into a drawer without bothering to sort or fold it, and sleeping on top of the bedspread so you won't have to make your bed in the morning.

If there's no one to notice, who cares if you chatter away to yourself, eat with your hands standing up or walk around the house in outfits that would scare babies?

The first thing I do when I get home is take off my make-up and good dress and put on a ratty robe and house slippers. It's like the reverse of a *Mademoiselle* make-over, but nobody is coming over to photograph me. It would be different were there a man in the house—and not just because I would have to wear decent clothes. Objects would no longer be where I put them. Radio dials would be turned, windows closed, ther-

19

mostats adjusted.

Of course, there is such a thing as compromise. Married people do it all the time. But one nice part about being single is that you don't have to accommodate anyone. Those of us with little idiosyncrasies rather like it that way.

The Perfect Man Wears Overalls

Something was chirping in my bedroom. The noise woke me up, though not as soon as it would have if I hadn't cleverly incorporated it into a dream about sparrows. No sound is pleasant in the middle of the night, but this one was particularly irritating. It consisted of a feeble chirp followed by silence, and—just when I thought it had stopped—another feeble chirp, like a bird on its last wing.

At times like this, I wish I didn't live alone. It would have been comforting to have had someone to turn to and ask, "What the hell is that?" A man would instantly have known where the noise was coming from and how to stop it. Men are good at fixing things that go chirp in the night.

Eventually I figured out what was chirping (my smoke detector; the battery was about to give out), just as I have figured out the source of various creaks, rattles and drips around my house. I have even repaired some of them myself.

I don't deny the satisfaction that comes from not having to rely on anyone else. But what none of us seemed to realize in our rush to learn home repair or home cooking or whichever skill would liberate us from dependence is that independence, too, has its drawbacks. The reality is that *two* people can solve a problem faster than *one*. *Two* can also laugh about a noise in the dead of night that *one* might not find so amusing.

Everyday living has become terribly complex. The more possessions we acquire and the more complicated those possessions become, the more frequently we have to cope with their breaking down. It is getting to the point where it almost takes two to cope. A lot of things have fallen apart on me lately. The smoke detector was the easiest to know what to do about. Because they all worked perfectly fine before I left on a trip, it reinforced my belief that gremlins get into your home when you're away. The TV screen had developed a wavy line that wouldn't go away despite my frantic attempts at fine tuning. The bathtub was draining at a rate of a drop a minute. The Cuisinart was threatening to explode when I turned it on, and the oven simply refused to get hot.

Whatever limited ability I have acquired with a screwdriver wouldn't have done any good, or so I thought. (One difference between the sexes is that women often assume a repair task is beyond them when it might not be, while men will attempt to fix almost anything.) I was more than willing to seek professional help. The problem was, I didn't know where to go to get it.

Take my television, please. It is hooked up to cable and a VCR. So should I summon the cable repairman or a person who fixes TVs or one who fixes VCRs? Maybe I could have all three of them come over and get a second and a third opinion. No wonder I longed to be able to divide the responsibility. *He* could take the TV and Cuisinart. *I* would attend to the bathtub and oven. I would have been grateful just to have someone to consult with on whom to call about the TV. It would have been a relief just to be able to bitch to another person that the Cuisinart came back from the shop in worse shape than when I brought it in.

In fairness, you should do the above only with a spouse or live-in mate, who would have a vested interest in getting the repairs made. I know how tempting it is to turn the person you are going out with into a handyman, especially if he or she happens to be at all handy. I've been guilty of this myself. But you risk making them feel like the hired help, which isn't exactly conducive to romance.

So that leaves us back where we started: alone and struggling to take care of things. And our plight has not gone unnoticed by comics, as this joke making the rounds illustrates:

Q: How does a single woman get rid of roaches in her apartment?
A: She asks them for a commitment.

I have my own version. It's not funny, but this is no laughing matter.

Q: How do single people handle life on their own?
A: The best they can.

Clipping and Saving the Best Meals You'll Ever Read

I am leafing through the food section of the paper with scissors poised. The Tuscan tomato soup sounds nice. Snip, snip. So does the poached shad roe with lemon butter. Snip, snip.

The less time I spend in the kitchen, the more time I seem to spend clipping recipes. When I used to cook regularly, it was from memory. Now that I mostly eat out, I have accumulated a recipe collection that would be the envy of Julia Child. Two big manila envelopes are stuffed with instructions for make-ahead French toast that I know I'll never make; pork chops with mustard and green peppercorn sauce or *à la mexicaine* or Normandy style that I won't serve any style; and a chilled peach soufflé that will never emerge from my kitchen.

I clip selectively, studying the ingredients and assembling them in my mind before deciding whether a particular dish is worthy. I can practically taste it before filing it away forever.

Occasionally, as I am about to rip a recipe out of a magazine that doesn't belong to me, I wonder about this odd habit of mine. I am like a boxer who hasn't been in the ring for ten years but still habitually tapes his hands. I suspect the recipes remind me of my glory days in the kitchen, when I would come home from work and whip up an elegant meal for two within an hour. I also did four-course dinner parties for eight, and brunches for twenty. I was quite a cook, or so my guests always said.

Shortly after I stopped being married, I stopped cooking. It wasn't really a conscious decision. It just happened.

I briefly tried following the advice of singles experts to cook for myself. I set the "table for one" with my good dishes, silver and crystal and even a candelabra. But I couldn't get into the spirit of it. With no one to compliment me, it didn't seem worth the effort. Also, I could never get the proportions right and would end up making enough for three and eating all of it.

I started eating out more and more often. I liked the feeling of having other people around even when I was by myself. Eating is such a sociable activity that it doesn't seem right to do it totally alone.

The longer I went without cooking, the more monumental the thought of entertaining became. Besides, my circle of friends changed. I no longer saw the couples with whom my husband and I had once exchanged dinner invitations. My single friends hardly ever cook—probably for the same reasons I don't.

My china began to collect dust in the cabinet. The silver got tarnished from disuse. The recipes started to pile up. Do I continue to clip them because I still delude myself that someday I will make those scrumptious-sounding dishes? Or do I clip as a substitute for making them? I suspect a little of both.

My feelings about cooking are all mixed up with leftover feelings about my marriage. They are bittersweet—like the recipe for bittersweet chocolate cake I couldn't stop myself from filing away for future reference.

Losing Money All by My Lonesome

I used to be a real flake about money. I would fall asleep while my then-husband and my then-accountant figured out my taxes. I'm not sure they noticed; that's how irrelevant I was to the proceedings. I had this notion there would always be money for whatever I wanted. And for a long time, there was.

When I was growing up, my doting mother allowed me to run up bills on her charge account, a practice she continued even when I was away at college. My husband would be furious when I bought yet another outfit, but none of the clothes was ever repossessed.

My metamorphosis from flake to fiscally responsible person started, as it has for many women, with a divorce. Suddenly I was paying the bills. I saw the correlation between what came in and what went out.

A few years later, my mother died and left me some money. I knew she was terrified I would blow all of it. For her sake as well as mine, I became determined to invest in something other than a new wardrobe. I may not have known much about financial management, but I did know how to shop. I compared ads for CDs until I found the one with the highest yield, locked up my money for two years at 13 1/2 percent and smiled when the statements came in.

However, as my account came due, interest rates tumbled. From everything I was reading, the stock market seemed the place to be. I liked the image of myself as someone who was in the market. But I was also scared. I've never been much of a gambler.

With some trepidation, I bought several newspaper stocks, because at least I was familiar with the product, and a mutual fund that, as the money magazines put it, had a solid ten-year record in both bull and bear markets. I took that to mean I had less chance of losing my shirt.

All my investments went up with dizzying speed. I loved calculating my profits. It made me feel so smart. This financial stuff was a breeze. Then the stock market crashed 508 points in one day. Staring at the tiny scraps on which I had written the amount of my windfall gave me a new understanding of the term "paper profit."

My first reaction was the same as the couple in the movie *Lost in America*, who, after gambling away all their savings in Las Vegas, asked the casino owner if he couldn't just give them their money back as a favor.

The helpless little girl in me emerged. Just as I would do when I used to spill my milk, I looked around for someone to blame. I wished I had a husband so I could have accused him. Men are supposed to know when to take money out of the market. What did I know about such things?

I felt as if I had been exposed for the flake I really am. Somebody should take away my checkbook and stop me before I invest again.

My confidence was even more shaky than the market, and I wondered if this was a normal reaction. When Gordon Getty's fortune was depleted by billions, did that make him question his ability to take care of himself? Gradually, I recovered, as did the market. I began to take stock.

I once had a friend who was always turning adversity into a learning experience. It got a bit tiresome hearing about what he had learned. Nonetheless, I have repeated a similar litany to myself. I have learned that to be in charge of your own life, you have to be responsible for your decisions. I chose to stay in the stock market. I took the credit, so I had to take the blame. I have learned that while it is nice to make money, my self-worth is not contingent on it.

I have learned never to brag about how well I'm doing in the market. My co-workers have suggested that I might want to make a dress out of the office draperies or dine at the local soup kitchen. That's O.K., guys, I deserve it.

And, finally, I have learned to be philosophical about all this, like the guy who owns the corner grocery by my house. When I stop in in the morning, he is glued to a tiny TV, watching the ticker on the financial news network. Once I asked him how the market was doing. "Up and down," he said. "Just like life."

Sometimes We All Need Someone

I came home in the middle of the day with a dizzying headache, chills and nausea, all the symptoms of what I used to call in my little-girl lisp the "fu." But no mommy was waiting at the door to feel my forehead with a reassuring palm, swaddle me in

25

blankets or feed me liquids and aspirin and, when I could stomach it, a little chicken soup.

Nobody was home to take care of me at all—not when I first stumbled into bed or at any point in the next twenty-four hours while the virus ran its bumpy course. Lying there in the dark, unable to sleep or get up, I felt sorry for myself because I was sick, and even sorrier because I was alone.

Illness brings out the worst fear that single people have: the possibility that they could be lying in bed or on a floor helpless and that no one would know or care.

I have a morbid memory for stories about people to whom this has happened. William Holden's body wasn't found for five days after he slipped on a throw rug and smashed his head on a table. If a famous movie star could go unmissed for that long, what hope is there for the rest of us?

At the same time, I'm aware how much of this fear is irrational. Most single people do have friends who know their whereabouts. At the very least, they have employers who would notice if they didn't come into work. The real problem is an unwillingness on the part of singles, myself included, to reach out to other people. If we don't tell anyone we're sick, then our worst fear *could* come true. But if we do, we sound needy, which is the last thing most of us want.

Being single—especially, I think, for women—is a declaration that you can take care of yourself. It's hard to temper that by acknowledging that maybe there are times when you can't. That wouldn't mean you were weak, just human.

Sure, there's a certain amount of wallowing that goes on. I imagine my friends off leading their busy lives and don't want to bother them to drive me to the doctor. It's hard for me to accept even when they offer. Instead, I suffer through it alone and eventually get well. I do what I suspect a lot of singles do. I go back to work too soon—tired of being at home, tired of being sick, but mostly tired of my own company.

I have no remedy for the ailment I have diagnosed. But I can offer some common-sense advice:

• Before you retire to bed for the duration, put everything you need—liquids, medication, telephone, TV—within arm's reach.
• Tell someone, preferably a neighbor, about your condition and arrange some sort of signal should you require assistance. If they can't hear you pounding on the floor, then ask them to call every couple of hours until you're through the worst of it.
• There's no reason to worry about food with so many grocery stores that deliver. It may cost a little extra, but when you're sick that is no time to pinch pennies.
• When your friends are at home alone with the flu, bring some juices or magazines over, even if they insist they don't need anything. Someday they may do the same for you.

A Quake Is No Time to Be Alone

I felt shaky even before the earthquake. I was in the midst of some serious self-analysis, trying to figure out why I always want to flee from secure relationships. What was I looking for, anyway? This was an inauspicious time to still be looking. If there's ever a night when you need someone to cling to, it's *after the earth literally moves.*

With no loved one—not to mention no electricity—in my apartment, I couldn't bear to stay there. I grabbed a flashlight (remembering that it had been a gift from a sweet man, who worried about how ill-equipped I was for an emergency, and thinking maybe I should have married him), checked that the quake hadn't done any real damage to my place and headed outside. I needed to be around people, even ones I didn't know.

A lot of other strays were wandering the streets of San Francisco. We sniffed each other out in the darkness and stopped to say a few reassuring words. Nobody asked how I came to be alone on this of all nights, nor did I ask anybody. But like me, they must have wondered. Couples walked by clasping hands as tightly as schoolchildren during a fire drill. I would have gotten married on the spot just to have a hand to hold that way.

I located a functioning pay phone and called my sister in Chicago. I longed to hear a loving voice. She said the family had been frantic with worry. That's wonderful, I thought.

She wanted me to move back to Chicago. At that moment, I think she meant it. Considering how alone I felt and the omnipresent fear of aftershocks, it didn't seem like such a bad idea.

In the next few days, dozens of people called from all over the country to make sure I was all right. I was touched by their concern. It made me realize I wasn't alone after all. Friends from the area checked in, too. Those with lights invited me to stay at their homes.

By then, however, I was doing O.K. in the dark. I had taken to falling asleep plugged into a transistor radio. It was a connection of sorts—although talk radio will never be a substitute for sweet talk.

The earthquake jolted me into seeing there is something wrong with the way I live. For instance, I didn't have to worry about food spoiling in the refrigerator because I don't keep any food there, or anywhere else in my kitchen. The jars of facial cream and dozen bottles of Évian water weren't likely to be affected by an electrical failure.

I decided I was tired of living like a hotel guest in my own home, and went out and spent $79 on serious groceries.

Subconsciously, I may have been preparing for another quake, although I prefer to think of it as finally settling in. I've been awakening at dawn every day since the quake and looking around. Why, my place has all the comforts of home. Funny I never noticed before. I definitely plan to spend more time there.

I am grateful it is intact and sorry for those who weren't so lucky.

It's my fault one man is temporarily homeless. Years ago, when we were briefly dating, I offered to find a new apartment for him. (I do things like that to impress men with what a good girl I am.) The place I found is in the neighborhood that was most seriously damaged by the quake. During my wanderings, I came across his building. It had been boarded up because of structural damage, and the tenants had yet to be allowed in. I felt terrible. I accept the responsibility for what happens during a relationship, which includes not intentionally hurting another person. But how can you predict the role you may *un*intentionally play in his or her life?

My worries the night of the quake seem pretty insignificant in the face of the death and disaster all around me. That's called perspective.

As reality sets in, the perspective becomes grander. My life has been changed in ways I'm not even aware of yet. I feel stronger for having gotten through it on my own. I'm emotionally drained. But, like the city I love, I'm still here.

MODERN ROMANCE

Remember when dating was something only teenagers did? Their mushy behavior and high anxiety could be excused by their tender age. Now a lot of us are acting like teenagers in love, though we're really too old for all that.

We have had to rewrite the rules of romance as we go along, starting with what to call the person you're dating. Boyfriend or girlfriend somehow doesn't sound right when said friend is forty-something. We've questioned how we're supposed to behave on a first date and even what qualifies as a date between consenting adults. As the romance heats up, there's more to confuse us. We look for help anywhere we can get it. We even consult soothsayers.

Meanwhile, sexual mores keep changing. The only hope is that with the right person and a little humor, we will somehow muddle through.

What Do You Call Your "Friend"? Try Using His Name

Bob Greene wrote a column lamenting that singles have no suitable term for the person with whom they are romantically involved. After dismissing "boyfriend" and "girlfriend" as juvenile and "lover" as creepy, he asked readers for their suggestions. Well, Bob, since you asked . . .

Dear Bob,

This just isn't the problem for singles that you seem to think it is. I, for one, have always known what to call the man with whom I am keeping company. I call him Tom or Dick or Harry, or whatever his name happens to be.

What you are really looking for is an equivalent of "my husband" or "my wife"—two words that will sum up this person's relationship to me. But why does he have to be "my" anything? Can't he just be himself?

In case you're wondering how that might work in a social situation, allow me to illustrate:

Suppose I were romantically linked with someone I'll call Sigmund Freud (not his real name). Now, suppose Sigmund and I run into you at a cocktail party, and I want to introduce the two of you. I would simply say: "Bob, I'd like you to meet Sigmund Freud. Sigmund, this is Bob Greene." If I were being expansive, I might add that you are a columnist and that he is, say, a shrink.

I would assume that Sigmund could carry his end of the conversation and that his connection to me would not be the most interesting thing about him. Sigmund is no groupie, you know. Being clever, you would probably figure out that Sigmund and I had something going without my having to spell it out.

Let's take another hypothetical situation: My girlfriends and I are gossiping about men and Sigmund's name comes up. "Who is this Sigmund?" they demand to know. I could reply, "He's my boyfriend/lover/companion," and leave it at that. But wouldn't it be better if I actually said something about him? Certainly that would mean more to my friends and be fairer to Sigmund.

"He is an absolutely fascinating man," I might say; "a little intense, but the best listener I've ever known. I feel like I could tell him anything."

Were I writing to my family about Sigmund, I could also easily avoid labeling him "my" whatever. I could indicate that he is someone special by mentioning the things we have done together. For example, "Sigmund and I have just returned from Vienna."

As you correctly point out, Bob, a lot more adults are staying single or becoming single again. In fact, 41 percent of the adult population is single. Many of us are struggling, but the struggle is not with the gaps in our vocabulary. We are trying to figure out how to go about having a relationship at an age when one should really be beyond all that.

We have been patterning ourselves after the most visible role models around: teenagers in love and married couples. From the former, we inherited the regrettable terms "dating," "boyfriend" and "girlfriend"; from the latter, we got the notion of appropriating another person, as if he or she belonged to us.

The reason singles have not had much success coming up with words for the person they love ("significant other" and "spouse equivalent" are not exactly catchy) is that they continue to look to married people as models. I say it is time for us to start doing things our own way. I suggest we begin by eliminating "my" from the vocabulary of romance.

This has a certain long-term advantage. By never referring to Sigmund as my boyfriend, should we break up, I will not be forced to call him my ex-boyfriend. He will always be simply Sigmund.

So there it is, Bob—not the snappy suggestion you had in mind, but, I would hope, a singular alternative:

Sincerely,
Ruthe

Mom Was Right—Just Be Yourself

I am a great believer in fate having a hand in romance. So when I ran into Paul at a museum, I took it as a sign that we could be meant for each other after all.

He and I had gone out a few times. I liked him, but there was an uneasiness between us that made me wonder after every date whether I would hear from him again and whether I even wanted to.

Then there we were: staring at the same watercolor at the same moment. Neither of us acted surprised, though the odds against meeting like this have to be astronomical. (Could it be Paul also believed in destiny? Funny, he didn't seem the type.) Since we were both alone, it seemed natural to wander around the museum together. It wasn't.

Paul, I couldn't help noticing, sprinted through the exhibits like O.J. Simpson at the airport. I followed along silently as he dashed from American Impressionism to African artifacts. But when he tried to see three thousand years of Asian art in thirteen minutes, I couldn't control myself any longer.

In the nicest way (or so I thought), I told him to slow down. I said that I had spent a lot of time in museums, and that he'd get more out of this one if he selected a few objects and really studied them instead of trying to look at everything. Paul waited for me to finish, and then let me have it. He said that I should stop telling him what to do, that he found me incredibly pushy and that that was why he wasn't rushing to ask me out again.

I've heard this sort of thing before from men, which may be why it didn't upset me. My guess is, Paul would have preferred if I had cried instead of smiling my Mona Lisa smile.

After our first date, the man I wound up marrying told me I was the most obnoxious woman he had ever been out with. There have been joking threats to throw me out of moving vehicles if I didn't shut up (to date, nobody has been driven to actually do it).

I prefer to think of myself as having a strong personality.

However, knowing this can be hard for some men to take, why don't I just rein it in and act more docile, at least in the beginning? I've been around enough to know that's really what most men want; they just give lip service to wanting a woman who speaks her mind.

In the early stage of a romance, there's always the question of how much of your true self you should reveal. It's like taking off your clothes for the first time. You worry whether the other person will find you pleasing.

While both kinds of stripping can be done with mirrors, I'm basically against subterfuge. You can't be anyone other than who you are for very long, so what's the point of even trying? I have a take-me-or-leave-me philosophy. As men find out if they stick around, I'm much better at relationships than I am at dating. I'm loyal, trustworthy and reasonably obedient—the Lassie of lovers.

To Paul, alas, I'm pushy and insensitive to his feelings. The latter was what he told me when I made the mistake of calling to see whether we couldn't talk about what had happened. We couldn't. And, in a sense, he's right. I knew that something about me bothered him and should have realized what it was before he had to tell me. But if I had realized, I'm not sure I would have done anything differently.

I've tried putting myself in his situation. How would I have responded to a lecture on Museum Walking 101?

Better than he did, that's for sure. But women are used to lectures from men. I've had Politics 101, Plumbing 101, Driving 101 and Investments 101, and I haven't minded as long as the lecturer seemed to know what he was talking about. I figure since you're going to be spending all that time together, why not learn from your date?

There are things I still have to learn in Dating 101, but I've got a good grasp of the basics. The fundamental basic is to like who you are and then wait for someone who likes you as much as you do.

Inside Scoop on Affairs of the Heart

I just wrote Maria, my astrologer friend, to ask how Scorpios and Libras make out in the long run. I've fallen for a Libra, and before I fall any further, I'd like a glimpse into our future. (I'd really like a panoramic view, but I hate sounding greedy.)

Maria is my key adviser on matters of the heart. I met her five years ago when I was in London. Every time I go back, she takes me on long walks in Kew Gardens and tells me whether I'm compatible with the man of the moment, as if he and I were computer software. When Maria talks, I listen. The world is a confusing place, especially the part of it inhabited by men. I figure if someone claims to have inside information, the least I can do is hear her out. After all, it can't hurt.

The times I've felt the need for reassurance and Maria has been far away, I've consulted others who claim intimate knowledge of my past, present and future. There are more of these advisers around than there used to be, probably because it's more confusing to be single than it used to be.

I resent being asked what's on my mind. That's what I expect *them* to tell *me*.

I also resent requests for an additional $20 for candles to be lit on my behalf. I would just as soon curse the darkness.

Offers to advise me on work and money matters are politely refused. I can handle all that myself. It's men who are the puzzlement.

A palmist once looked into my hand and told me to stick with my current beau. I couldn't help wondering if she said that to everyone, figuring a man in hand is always worth two in the wild.

As far as I can tell, the prediction of a tarot card reader that I would find happiness with a Libra, Taurus or Pisces has already come true. And practically everything Maria has said turned out to be accurate, I suspect because it came from the heart as well as astrological charts. However, *other* advice has been so far off that

I've questioned whose future was being peered into. For example, the tea leaf reader who warned me to beware of girlfriends' trying to steal my man obviously doesn't know my girlfriends.

I've never made any major changes suggested by spiritual advisers. But I like being privy to their information, anyway. I figure knowing about it can't hurt.

I kept my opinion to myself a few years ago while trying to uncover the identity of the San Francisco astrologer who advised the Reagans on the presidential schedule. I managed to track her down—my biggest scoop in twenty-five years of journalism. I laughed along with the cynical editors who were amazed that Nancy Reagan and possibly the president put any credence in this stuff. How could I say what I really thought: that it couldn't hurt?

Thinking this way is in my genes. I come from a family with a direct pipeline to inside information. So what if most people would call it nothing more than superstition?

My mother had heard that black cats and open ladders were bad luck. She never claimed this to be a fact. But, she would say, it couldn't hurt to steer clear of them just in case. When she would notice me with a button about to fall off, she insisted I chew a piece of thread while she sewed it back on. She had heard it would prevent her from sewing up my brains. I never asked whether she really believed that was a serious risk. But if I had, I'm sure she would have said, "Who knows? But it can't hurt to chew."

The other day, I went to a Russian seamstress to replace a button that had popped off at work. When she started to sew on me, I instinctively grabbed some thread. She saw it go into my mouth and smiled her approval. She understood exactly what I was doing and why. I wouldn't be surprised if her relatives got this particular inside information in the same Russian village as mine. "It can't hurt," she said.

Every day now, I check the mail for a reply from London. My future with Libra is looking very bright. Still, I'm eager to know what Maria has to say. Why not? It can't hurt.

Saying Less Is More on a First Date

"So, tell me about yourself." For all the times I've been asked that by men who were as much strangers to me as I was to them, I'm still not sure how to respond. On a first date, I am like the "Great Gatsby," willfully re-creating myself to please another person. But which facts—or fictions—are likely to do the trick?

When I was younger and had less to tell, I told more. Men I never heard from again were privy to intimate details of my life. Maybe that was why they didn't call back—not that the details were so sordid, but it must have seemed there wasn't much else to know.

I learned from experience what to leave out, beginning with any mention of other men. Believe me, I understand how tempting it is to go on about past relationships. You're trying to impress this other person with how desirable you are when that may be far from the way you're feeling. But your "And then I went out with" monologue is likely to annoy your date and make him think twice about going out with you again. What man would want his name added to such a long list?

I do, however, talk about my ex-spouse. He is too much a part of my past to make disappear. But I delete the bit about the messy divorce. I've come to realize that any material that would play on a psychiatrist's couch is not appropriate on a first date.

I edit out anything that doesn't conform to the image I am trying to create of myself. I like to let drop the fact that I flew to New York just to see *Nicholas Nickleby*, for instance, because it makes me appear cultured and energetic. However, I skip over the man who was waiting for me there, lest it seem I was more interested in him than Dickens.

Probably I spend too much time talking about work. It's such familiar ground and so safe. Also, I happen to have a job that, if I choose to lay it on, sounds awfully glamorous—which is the image I want. I have actually sat a new man down with a scrapbook of newspaper articles I've written. Here I am with Princess Grace in Monaco, with Prince Charles in England, with Melina Mercouri in Greece. And all the while I am thinking, "God, I must sound insufferable. Why isn't this poor guy making a dash for the door?"

A first date is not a job interview. You are not obligated to account for every year of your life. Nobody is going to check your references. You are, at least for the moment, exactly who you say you are.

I've resisted the inevitable temptation to lie. Well, O.K., I've fudged a little on my running time. But I have never knocked any years off my age. Even as the men have gotten younger, I have not. When a man asks me about myself, what he gets is the true story filtered through gauze. In my version, I am always the heroine. I am unfailingly charming and self-possessed. I never do stupid things. Listening to me go on, how could any man *not* like me?

But if one were to listen carefully, he'd hear the shaky voice under the strong one. It's saying: "See beneath the bravado. See me."

Delicious Way of Getting Acquainted

If Shakespeare were single today, he never would have alluded to music being the food of love. Like the rest of us, he would have known that the real food of love is food.

Think about what you have done on the last dozen dates. I'd be willing to bet dinner that more than half of them involved serious dining, and that you had a snack on the others. So much of the dating game is played at a table for two, because it's the most palatable way to get to know one another. You can eat and talk at the same time. (Well, maybe not while your mouth is full— remember Mom's advice—but certainly between morsels.)

Now that sex has been put on the back burner, you will likely become intimate with your date's dietary habits long before you're intimate with your date.

I can live with, or at least dine with, men who have given up meat. However, when they start giving up dairy products and inquiring whether the broth the soup is made from is animal or vegetable, I begin to develop heartburn.

Dining together provides a glimpse of the kind of person you're out with. But you have to pay attention. For instance, I always notice how a man treats the help at a restaurant. If he orders waiters around, I figure someday he'll do the same to me.

I also notice if he's proprietary about his food—a mark, I have come to believe, of an ungenerous spirit. In my family, everybody sampled what everybody else had ordered; that was half the fun of eating out. I still ask, "Wanna taste?" before I've had one myself. A man who guards his plate like a catcher at home plate strikes out with me.

I don't grade down for table manners, probably because mine aren't so hot. But if such things matter to you, it's better to discover sooner than later that your companion eats peas with a knife or drinks from the finger bowl.

Each meal has its own special place in the dating and mating ritual. The order of importance isn't what it would be if nourishment were all the two of you had in mind.

Lunch is for getting acquainted. It's more like an audition for a date than an actual date. A woman can ask a man to lunch without fear of usurping his role. You can flirt wildly, knowing that nothing can come of it, at least not that afternoon, because you're both expected back at the office. If there's no chemistry, you can return to your respective cubicles without having to endure that embarrassing moment on a real date when one person tries to kiss the other good night.

However, be aware that there's no such thing as an *innocent* lunch. Married people who think it's O.K. to have a midday repast with someone they're attracted to may find themselves in the soup.

Dinner is a serious commitment of your time and money. Extending an invitation is your way of saying you think this person is worth both. If you're going to do it, do it right. Put some thought into the restaurant. Seek out romantic places—soft lights, flowers, a waiter with a French accent—and avoid ones where you won't be able to hear each other over the crowd.

I'd suggest a leisurely meal instead of rushing off to a movie or concert. Remember what the point is: to be learning about one another. And, though having your date over for dinner is a delicious idea, it should be tabled until you're certain that what you have cooking is a relationship.

Breakfast is as intimate as eating together gets—even if you haven't spent the night before together. Mornings are a time for no makeup and no pretense, when you are the closest to being who you really are. You have to be sure about another person to be willing to let him or her see you unadorned.

I can't think of anything nicer than a languorous morning with the lingering smell of bacon and eggs (oat bran and wheat germ for you purists) and the Sunday paper spread out on the table.

Congratulations. You've reached the point after all those getting-to-know-you meals when you no longer feel a need to keep talking. You can say it all with a look or a simple, "Can I get you anything, dear?"

It's Not Easy for Singles to Act Their Age

I got it into my head a few months ago that I should date around. A romance had come to an end, and a time-out from intense involvements seemed in order. I didn't want to care that way about anyone. I envisioned myself as the Carefree Single, a counterpart to Jeanette MacDonald's "Merry Widow" and Ginger Rogers' "Gay Divorcee."

My plan had not progressed very far when I met a man who torpedoed it. While still trying to resist his charms—orchids after the first date delivered to my office so everybody could see them, for instance—I attempted to explain my wanderlust to him. "You're right," he said with mock solemnity. "Dating around is exactly what every forty-four-year-old woman ought to be doing."

Until then, I hadn't considered I might be too old for this sort of thing. It had to be pointed out to me by someone from an older generation who had grown up with the notion that there was a time for everything.

We baby boomers have no sense of what's appropriate behavior for people our age (which may explain why we're carrying the tag "baby" into middle age and, presumably, beyond). We've done things pretty much willy-nilly. If a book about life's passages were written just about us, there wouldn't be any order to it. Mine is the generation that postponed marriage so long that couples old enough to be grandparents are just now getting around to having their first kid!

Those of us who continue to resist parenthood may never develop a realistic sense of how old we are. Children have a habit of growing up. They're a continual reminder of time slipping by; without them, the slippage can easily go unnoticed. And thanks to exercise and better diets, people don't *look* their age anymore, which makes it even harder to act it. When I go shopping, I find myself dismissing clothes as too "old" for me, though I can't seriously believe the designer had a sixty-year-old in mind. I've yet to run across anything I thought was too youthful.

As a result of sweating my way through aerobics classes, I've developed acne alongside my wrinkles. No wonder, like many others of my generation, I'm a little confused about how I should behave.

Nowhere is this confusion more evident than when it comes to dating. The conversations I have had with my girlfriends about men aren't much different from the ones I had when I was fifteen. We are still wrestling with those momentous teenage questions: How far should you go on the first date? Will he call when he says he will? If he doesn't, what do you do?

Men, to hear them tell it, still get sweaty palms at the thought of calling a woman, and are no more sure than they were in high school whether their date really means it when she says, "No."

Every generation has had its share of single people past their prime. If you think back, you can probably recall a maiden aunt or bachelor uncle in your family tree. Perhaps there was even a widow or divorcee, who was unlikely to have been either merry or gay. If they went out at all, it was a discreet fix-up engineered by a relative who felt sorry for them. Usually, nothing came of it. These people accepted their station in life; they weren't trying to change it.

Certainly, they didn't flaunt their singleness by taking out personal ads. Had they disclosed to anyone a desire to date around, they would have been looked at as if they had a screw loose.

Here's what I wonder: Should we be more like Aunt Tillie or Uncle Nick? Should we act our age instead of acting like teenagers? Should we really be dating around?

Not having done the latter for a long time, I may have romanticized what it is like. My girlfriends tell me it's a jungle out there, that the ratio of jerks to nice guys is about 10 to 1. Still, if a relationship is what you're looking for, you have to start somewhere. Dating around should be a means to an end, not, as I imagined, an end in itself. I'm glad I found a nice man to remind me of that.

Why Women Should Wait for His Call

There is nothing like waiting for a man to call to zap you of your power. You could be involved in arbitrage or run a corporation or perform brain surgery—and still be transformed into a jellyfish by a telephone that resolutely refuses to ring. It might seem the more successful you were, the less it would matter what one man thinks of you (or that he isn't thinking of you: the real message of a silent phone communicates).

However, the empowerment of women has not made them immune to caring. If anything, having control over part of your life lulls you into thinking you can control all of it, so you're *more* susceptible to being hurt. After all, when it comes to motivating the opposite sex, you really can't do anything. You can make money and decisions and employees quiver in your wake, but you cannot make a man pick up a phone.

I have a friend who is learning this the hard way. I'll call her Dotty; that's not her name, but it describes how she has been driven to feel.

Dotty, who is notoriously fussy about men (with her six-figure salary as a corporate V.P., she can afford to be), finally went out with

45

someone she found exciting. They spent eight charmed hours together, in the course of which he told her she was beautiful, smart, unique and sexy, and made a few observations about her body she is embarrassed to repeat even to me.

She couldn't wait to hear from him again, but waiting is just what she has been forced to do.

The first week after their date, every time she heard the phone, she was convinced it was her sweet-talking man. However, the voice on the line wasn't the one she was pining after. Now that the weeks are stretching into a month, she is confused and angry—at herself as much as at him. "I'm staring at a phone when I should be working. I can't believe how I've let him get to me," she laments.

Men are wrong if they think women never consider calling them. Dotty has thought about almost nothing else. She sees telephones everywhere she goes. But she can't quite bring herself to dial his number.

"I guess I have too much pride," she admits. "Also, I honestly don't know what I would say. If I try him at his office, I'll have to go through a secretary who will no doubt ask me what this is regarding. What do I tell her: 'It's regarding the fact that your boss led me on'?"

Women in Dotty's situation are not completely helpless. There are always ploys to remind your gentleman non-caller of your existence.

You could write him a coy note, ostensibly to tell him about a new book you thought he might be interested in. You could arrange an accidental meeting or cajole a mutual friend to mention your name, preferably in every other sentence. However, these things are pretty transparent. Men may be thoughtless, but they're not stupid.

My own feeling is you should do nothing and wait it out, even if the wait turns out to be in vain. Men have an instinctive need to make the first several moves. It's probably left over from caveman days. As exasperating as it may be for women accustomed to taking action at work, you have to let a guy come to you in the beginning—

or risk humiliation far worse than a still phone.

Whenever I'm tempted to call a man, I reread Dorothy Parker's classic short story "A Telephone Call." From the opening line—"Please, God, let him telephone me now,"—you know the author has been there. Take to heart her other words: "When you do [telephone them], they know you are thinking about them and wanting them, and that makes them hate you."

I don't know why Dotty hasn't heard from her man, and it looks as if she and I may never find out. If he were confronted, he would make up an excuse anyway, such as he got swamped at the office or misplaced her number or came down with amnesia. However, the basic reason he and other men fail to phone is: They don't want to.

This may not be the call you've been waiting for, but it has the ring of truth.

Stand Up to Whoever Stands You Up

The play ended much earlier than I had thought, and I had an hour until I was to meet my date for dinner. Since the restaurant was nearby, I decided to wait there.

I explained the circumstances to the maître d', who, without hesitating, showed me to a table. He didn't even blanch when I took out a book. However, a half-hour later he was back with a menu. "Would madam like to order now?" he asked. I explained, again, that I was waiting for somebody. "Perhaps you would like to order anyway, in case the somebody doesn't show up," he replied.

His concern for me wasn't personal. It was business. Presumably, he'd had his share of customers run out of the restaurant when it became apparent they had been stood up. By getting me to order, at least he could present me with a bill on my way out.

I resisted the urge to protest that, of course, my date would show up. However, when he arrived at precisely the agreed-upon time, I shot the maître d' an I-told-you-so look.

It has been so long since I've been stood up, I almost forgot that sort of thing happens. This episode reminded me. It also got me thinking of ways to assure you are never left waiting for Godot, or any other notorious no-show. The most obvious way is to avoid anyone who would be capable of such contemptible behavior.

If you have developed any sense about people—and it's dangerous to be dating, if you haven't—you should be able to tell the jerks from the good ones. But sometimes the jerks can fool you or prove so irresistible that you overlook their jerkiness.

The only time I *was* stood up, it was because I ignored an inner warning that I was dealing with a major-league jerk. His name was André. He was a filmmaker, who, when we met, had just won an Academy Award. I realize now I was more enthralled with Oscar than André; nonetheless, I can't deny I was enthralled.

After several dates, we were to meet one night at a restaurant. My dinner with André never took place.

When he was five minutes late, I got this sinking feeling that he wasn't going to show, as if I had known all along it would come to this. I waited a half-hour, thinking he would at least call. But, being a jerk, he never did.

My worst-case scenario was that André would become a famous producer—as he kept telling me he was going to be—and I would have to read about him in the paper. However, as far as I know, he never made another film. I hope he ended up waiting tables in Hollywood and that he's regularly stiffed by customers who have been stood up.

If you have ever waited anywhere in vain, my advice is: Don't even think of giving the no-show a second chance. Tell him or her you're not interested in an explanation, because no explanation (short of having been in an accident on the way to meet you and winding up in intensive care) could excuse that kind of gross inconsideration.

The reason you shouldn't go out with him or her again isn't only that you risk being stood up a second time (which you will be, and a third and a fourth). A person who is capable of standing you up is capable of anything. He or she will break your heart or steal your money or mess up your life in ways you can't even fathom.

You should almost be grateful for being stood up, especially if it happens early in a relationship. It's like a warning signal flashing: Get rid of this jerk.

The longer I've been dating, the more I gravitate toward men I can count on unfailingly. After all, that's how I am. If I say I'm going to meet someone, you can bet your savings account on it. Why shouldn't I expect the same in return?

If you have that in another person, no maître d' is ever going to intimidate you. Just look him in the eye and say your somebody always shows up!

When You're the One Who Loves More

In all the romances I can think of, including my own, there has been an imbalance. And unless it becomes hopelessly lopsided, it's good for a relationship. Things would get pretty boring if you both cared equally for each other at all times. Even Juliet, whose feelings hardly went unrequited, loved too much too soon. Her "wherefore art thou" speech sounds desperate to me. However, in the end, Romeo was more possessed than she. Remember, he killed himself for real first.

A wise older woman once told me it is always better to be the one who is loved more. I have come to understand what she meant. It is an incredibly secure feeling, bordering on smugness, to know you have that kind of hold over someone. But for sheer excitement, I recommend teetering on the other end of the love seesaw—a position I have been in a few times myself.

A perverse psychology comes into play. The less interested the other person seems, the more alive with feelings you become. That can be a delicious high, at least in the short run.

Following this logic, you could probably get someone to fall for you simply by holding back. However, I'm incapable of doing so when I really care, and what would be the point if I didn't? My style is to rush right in and make a fool of myself: a Fool for Love, if you please.

I've done some pretty stupid things. My most embarrassing moment, which you'll never read about in *Reader's Digest*, occurred when I was newly single, a vulnerable time for everyone.

I was convinced I had met the man of my dreams, not realizing it doesn't happen that quick. This guy's ardor cooled as mine heated up. Of course, that only made him more desirable. On my way back from a trip, I got an irresistible urge to call him from the airport and confess my most intimate thought. (Never a good idea, I have since learned.) He didn't sound all that happy to hear from me, but I went blithely on. I believe my exact words were "God, I really want you." There was silence on the other end. Suddenly it dawned on me he wasn't alone. (Indeed, he was in bed with another woman.)

I'm no longer quite this impulsive. I have learned to protect myself, to get out when the imbalance seems unlikely to ever tip in my favor again, and when the relationship starts to resemble a "fatal attraction."

I am also finally able to enjoy having men adore me, rather than being made uncomfortable by it or questioning their judgment.

The ups and downs of romance are inevitable. Feelings change; sometimes they swing back, and sometimes they don't. There's not much you can do about the latter except be honest with each other. You shouldn't hang on to a relationship when the feeling is gone. It's tempting to cling, because you don't know whether you'll ever find anyone else. But a person is not a security blanket.

I can forgive almost anything except deliberate dishonesty— toying with someone's emotions for what seem to me immoral purposes. An obvious example is a man who pretends to care to get a woman to sleep with him. The "I love you" line, or even a modified "I really like you," sounds pretty hollow when spoken too soon.

A girlfriend was once pursued by a much older man, who wrote her wonderfully steamy love letters. When she became as enamored as she assumed *he* was, he disappeared without a phone call, let alone a letter. I think he was using her to make himself feel young. Women are just as guilty of this kind of dishonesty. Often they do it to prove they are desirable to men—or simply to come alive.

Feelings get trampled on, even when that's not the intention. The delicate imbalance of a love affair winds up off-kilter, and nothing can be done to set it right. So whichever end of the love seesaw you happen to be on, you might as well enjoy the ride while it lasts.

Live Apart If You Can't Say "I Do"

I have never understood why people would live together as man and wife if they were not actually married. To share a home seems so intimate—even more so than sharing a bed—that if I were ready to make such a commitment to someone, I would go ahead and marry him.

If I didn't want to marry him, why in the world would I want to live with him? And if he didn't want to marry me, why should I be with him night and day? I'm not interested in merging my laundry or my finances with a significant other. If I needed help paying off my mortgage, I'd take in a boarder before I'd take in a boyfriend.

I don't buy the theory that living together is a good way to tell whether you are suited for marriage. It's not the same thing when you know you can move out as easily as you moved in. A legal document ties you together—if not until death do you part, at least until the divorce becomes final.

My gut feeling that cohabiting is no guarantee of marital bliss has been confirmed by a study that was reported in papers around the country. It found that couples who lived together before marrying have nearly an 80-percent-higher divorce rate than those who did not. While the researchers were careful to say they have no evidence that cohabiting causes higher divorce rates, it certainly doesn't seem to be doing anything to bring them down.

51

The women I know who shacked up with their boyfriends regretted it later, not because it failed to produce a happy marriage, but because it produced no marriage at all.

My friend Sara, for instance, wanted to marry the guy she had been dating for two years, but he wasn't interested. She finally persuaded him to move in with her, thinking that would convince him he couldn't live without her. He became enamored, all right—but with her apartment building instead of her. He broke up with Sara, bought the building and moved in across the hall from her with his new girlfriend. That was more than Sara could bear. Her live-in arrangement cost her not just a boyfriend, but a perfectly fine apartment as well.

Suppose you have better luck than Sara, and you and your housemate do end up getting married. You'll know everything there is to know about each other and deprive yourselves of the mystery of being newlyweds.

I am not so naive that I envision a virginal wedding night. But it's one thing to have slept together and quite another to have lived together. It's hard to have any illusions left when you've listened to your bride or groom snore every night for a year or watched them floss their teeth. I know a couple who came home early from their honeymoon. They'd lived together so long they were bored with each other's company.

I've seen too many friends march down the aisle like old married folks. They leave their own house with the TV and the VCR and the microwave and then go home again after the ceremony. Their wedding guests are at a loss to know what to buy them because they have everything they need. Setting up house becomes a ruse when you've already been playing house.

Some singles go from living with one person to another to another. They call it love; I call it dependency. They seem so afraid of being alone that any warm body is better than no body.

I would think it would be creepy staying in an apartment with the ghosts of so many past lovers. I have a friend who keeps coming across books and record albums he knows he never bought. The trouble is, he no longer can remember who they belong to so he could return them.

After one divorce, my faith in happy-ever-after endings has been shaken. But I don't see how you can enter into a live-in relationship with the attitude of "Well, let's see if this works out." You have to *believe* that it will work out. The best way to convince yourself and the person you love is to say, "I do," first, and move in later.

'70s Thrills Turn to '80s Chills

I once met an extremely engaging man at a party that friends had taken me to in Washington, D.C. He and I had all sorts of things to say to each other, and we had chemistry—a combination that in my experience has been pretty rare. We chattered away for hours. But when the party started to break up, instead of suggesting we go somewhere else or asking how he could get in touch with me, he excused himself and took off.

I was desperate to see him again, and fast, since I was leaving town in a few days. Being in a strange city without any of my contacts for tracking down men at home, I used the only resource I could think of: the telephone book.

Sure enough, he was listed, along with his address. I could have just called and suggested we get together. Instead, I got the idea of appearing at his doorstep in the middle of a Sunday afternoon. I thought he would be surprised. He was surprised, all right, and so was the woman he lived with. To his credit, he invited me in. The three of us made small talk for as long as I could bear it. As he walked me to the door, he whispered, "You were very brave to come over here like this."

"Crazy" was more like it. But in 1979, when this incident happened, everybody I knew was taking crazy risks. The '70s were such a crazy time to be single that crazy seemed normal. It was a time when *anything* went.

If I were to meet that man today, there's no way I would show up at his house unannounced. I'd be afraid to.

The mood among singles has changed. We have become generally afraid: afraid of getting AIDS, afraid of a fatal attraction, afraid of being a person who loves too much. There is a sort of obsession with playing it safe, and I don't just mean when it comes to sex. People don't want to put themselves on the line anymore. They've been hurt too many times. Instead of making the first move, they wait to be approached.

Many times, they wait in vain.

The prudent side of me says that's probably just as well. Better safe than sorry, and all that. But my other side—the side that remembers how much fun it was to be a little out of control—misses the nuttiness.

It's a kick to run the equivalent of an FBI check on someone you have just met to gather information for your pursuit. It is thrilling to find out where he or she is going to be at a particular time and arrange an accidental meeting. It makes your heart pound to call a stranger you saw across a crowded room, intending to ask him or her out; and the adrenaline rush only intensifies if you chicken out and hang up at the sound of a voice.

For a while, I thought maybe it was just the baby-boom generation which had gotten too old for all this. But singles in their twenties don't seem to want to put themselves out, either.

F. Scott Fitzgerald once wrote that there are two kinds of people: the pursued and those who do the pursuing. These days, it seems everybody wants to be the former. But those of us who have been the pursuers don't regret it, no matter how outrageous it got.

My friend Sally once found out where the man she was after would be changing planes. She met his flight wearing a trench coat over a negligee and carrying a bottle of champagne. He was charmed, though not charmed enough to fall in love with her.

When she thinks back on that time, it is with pleasure. So what if it didn't work out? She had fun. I still remember how I felt ringing that doorbell in Washington, D.C. I felt alive. Isn't that what it's all about?

HOW YOU MEET SOMEBODY

The search for the Holy Grail has nothing over the search for the elusive someone. How singles connect with one another appears to be a mystery to most singles. The single question I get asked most often is: How do I meet someone? I wish I had a magic formula for making your someones appear like genies. But it's not that simple. Like everything else in life, you have to work at it.

You need to call attention to yourself any way you can, from flirting outrageously to wearing a miniskirt in public. You should hound your friends to fix you up and go where members of the opposite sex are likely to be, including, if you can handle them, singles parties.

It's distressful to finally connect with someone, only to have that person disappear into the crowd. Could he or she have been your special someone? You'll never know.

Forget Mother's Advice, Talk to Strangers

Singles keep asking me the same question, whether it comes wrapped in a short life history, shrouded in euphemisms or surrounded by awkward "Ums," "Uhs" and "Buts": "How do I meet someone?"

The obvious answer is to go where members of the opposite sex are likely to be.

Christmas or Father's Day, for instance, provide women with a perfect excuse to hang out at men's stores. But once they are there—and this brings me to a more subtle answer—they have to figure out what to do next.

What I would do is look around for a man I'm attracted to and ask his opinion of a particular tie. If he seems friendly, keep talking and see what develops. Of course, there's always the chance nothing will develop. But you'll never know if you don't take a chance. By the same token, I can lead you to restaurant counters—breakfast on the weekends is a relaxed time to try to meet someone—but unless you get up the courage to ask the man or woman next to you about a front-page story, all you'll end up with is the check.

I can even direct you to 10K races, where you'll run up against lots of sweaty men and women in great physical shape. But if you can't bring yourself to compare times with one of them, you may as well stay home and run in place.

What I'm saying is that you are not going to get anywhere unless you're willing to put yourself on the line. If you are willing to do so, you can meet people at the corner grocery store.

I have met men at the symphony, at the movies, on the street. I've been asked how come I'm not afraid to talk to strangers, but

I'll take my chances with a stranger who goes to the symphony over one who haunts singles bars any day. The real fear isn't that someone is going to harm you, but that he or she will look at you like you're crazy or, worse yet, like you aren't there.

If you worry about words failing you when you're face-to-face with an attractive stranger, put them in writing. I have a friend who wound up marrying a man who wrote her a mash note on the inside of a matchbook cover the first time they met.

I have more calculated ways to meet the opposite sex:

• If you have reason to suspect an event is going to sell out, such as a championship game, buy an extra ticket in advance. Then sell it the night of the event to a ticket-less person of your choice. You'll have to sit next to each other for a couple of hours, and you'll have an obvious subject to discuss.

• If you see an interesting-looking person reading a book in a café, dash over to the nearest bookstore and buy a copy of the same book. Seat yourself at a nearby table and, with an incredulous smile, point out the coincidence.

• If you find yourself in the meat department next to someone you wouldn't mind sharing a steak with, start up a conversation with the butcher. You might complain about how no one ever makes dinner for you and see if the hint is picked up.

• If you can't seem to get the eye of someone in your office you're dying to meet, have yourself paged so you have to walk by his or her desk. Of course, you will only want to do this on days when you look sensational.

These methods don't always work. But they're worth a shot. At least you'll feel as if you're doing something to meet that elusive someone, instead of just complaining.

For Maxi Attention, Wear a Mini

Psssst! Want to know how to meet men? Get yourself a mini-skirt—the shorter, the better. What the fashion industry hasn't been telling you in its campaign to get women to hike up their hems is the effect that this has on the opposite sex.

I learned of it firsthand the night I put on a skirt so short that bending over suddenly became a moral decision. I chose to make my debut at the symphony. I mean, anyone can sneak into a darkened movie house with most of her thighs showing.

But to negotiate the endless rows at a symphony hall, aware that when you say, "Excuse me," nobody is watching your lips, and then cross one exposed leg over the other to the familiar "bum, bum, bum, bumm" of Beethoven's Fifth—now that takes courage.

I was, however, rewarded for my effort. During intermission, three men told me I was looking good and a fourth offered to buy me a drink. It's possible he may have thought I needed it. Later, at a crowded restaurant, the line parted when I came in. I was honked at repeatedly walking back to my car. One driver actually pulled over to the curb. I suspect he had something other than coffee in mind.

How did I feel about all this attention? Frankly, I reveled in it. After years of wanting men to admire my mind, I realized it was more gratifying to have them admire my legs. Of course, I wouldn't have dared appear in a mini if it weren't being touted as the latest fashion. The top designers have made the tramp look respectable, so that it is now possible to spend hundreds of dollars on looking cheap. I say, go for it!

For some inexplicable reason, feminism induced guilt in women for so much as thinking about dressing sexy. Then along came the big push to "make it in a man's world," and, with that, the perfectly dreadful dress-for-success business suit. I interpreted it as a tiny rebellion when some women began unbuttoning one too many buttons on their color-coordinated silk blouses.

Short skirts have finally given women back their sexuality, which they seemed to have placed in a blind trust while climbing the corporate ladder. Whether they would have gotten to the top faster in a mini is anyone's guess.

The question now is: Should you or shouldn't you hoist up your hemline and, if so, how much? There's an attempt to make age and/or the condition of your knees and thighs the determining factor. But it seems to me that marital status may be more pertinent—especially since I suspect a lot of men aren't going to want their wives running around with their underpants showing.

The miniskirt could become a way of signaling that you're available, in the same sense that in Polynesia a flower worn over the right ear indicates a woman is single. If you're game to show your gams, here are some things you should know:

• Begin by experimenting with different lengths. I would take an old skirt and just keep shortening it. Start at two inches above the knee—anything less than that is not much of a statement—and inch your way up.
• Forget about trying to find a slip short enough to go under your mini. Remember, the whole point is less clothes.
• You have to walk around as if there is nothing unusual about your attire. Don't even consider tugging at your hem. That won't make it grow; it will only make you look foolish.
• Think of your miniskirt as bait. Once you have hooked a guy, he'll have plenty of time to see there's more to you than meets the eye.

Dual-Minded Reason to Go Back to School

I have had several calls from girlfriends who want to tell me, not about a new man—which is what I expected from the excited tone of their voices—but about a new course they have discovered.

They phoned to find out if I was interested in taking it with them. While their classes did sound enticing (especially the ones on Beethoven's symphonies and James Joyce), I declined because I had already signed up to study Renaissance art. Having stared for hours at the Raphaels, Michelangelos and Botticellis all over Italy, I'm curious to learn what I overlooked.

My friend who will be reading Joyce told me she hopes to fill the "black holes" in her education. Later she acknowledged, sounding embarrassed, as if it detracted from her quest for knowledge, that she also hopes to meet men in class. Both motives strike me as noble: Joyce, from what I've read of him, would have approved.

I get an urge every September to go back to school, a Pavlovian response from all the years when that was what I did. If, however, you're like this friend and need the thought of droves of eligible singles to get you into a classroom again, then be assured you will find them. Many of the students in continuing education are unattached. (The super-moms and super-dads are all home in the evening spending "quality time" with their kids.)

I sense a readiness among more singles for this kind of extracurricular activity. We've wasted enough time on our obsession with being single, as if that were a serious subject worthy of study instead of what it is: a box to check under marital status.

We have gone so far as to create our own literature. It is my hope that we are ready to move beyond those advice manuals with the double-decker titles—which I generically call *Women Who Love the Men Who Hate Women Too Much*—to books we can actually learn from. In a sense, Joyce was writing about the same thing, the difference being that he had something to say.

I have had wonderful experiences taking classes as an adult. There is something both virtuous and luxurious about learning for its own sake. The semester I studied Joseph Conrad, Francis Ford Coppola came to class. He was a neighbor of the teacher's, and when he heard she was going to be lecturing on *Heart of Darkness*, he asked if he could attend.

As it turned out, he didn't want to listen to her. He wanted to talk about his theories of *Heart of Darkness*—a novel that fascinated him so much that he would base *Apocalypse Now* on it. The hilarious part was that most of the students didn't know who he was. They complained, at break, about the fat guy who had missed all the other classes and was monopolizing this one.

The way my interests have changed has been reflected in the subjects I've pursued. In the early '70s, I was heavy into extrasensory perception. Then I went through my literary stage.

After my divorce, I decided to become a responsible adult and took courses on financial planning, which were so boring that I retreated back to novels. I'll never get rich studying them, but they have other rewards.

There seems to be a trend in adult education to teach people things they can do something with. Leafing through one catalog, I noticed an abundance of classes with practical titles such as Sales Management and Accounting Basics for Non-Accountants. I admit I prefer nonpractical courses.

But getting back to meeting someone (I haven't forgotten, and I doubt that you have, either), think of it this way: You can predetermine the kind of person you'll encounter by the course you select.

What dating service can guarantee you a mate with whom you can discuss *Ulysses,* or even the basics of accounting? Talk about having something in common. I am not promising you will connect with a classmate or your money back. But I do promise you will learn something. And that really does have its own rewards.

The Distant Allure of Sailors

Accompanied by my friend Suzy, who was all of five feet tall but talked big, I spent many a Saturday evening when I was a teenager looking for sailors along State Street, the very same great street Frank Sinatra sings about. Suzy and I would douse ourselves with perfume and hair spray and parade back and forth, whispering conspiratorially to each other, until we were seen, if not smelled.

We were so amazed at our cheekiness that sometimes we would dissolve into giggles. But, oh, it was fun to be testing our charms. There was such a sense of power when one, or preferably two, of the sailors noticed us.

Most of what I know about flirting came from those experiences. It is enough that I have never had to take a class on how to flirt.

I learned how to stare and quickly look away so a guy can't be sure whether you've got your eyes on him or not. I learned to use a girlfriend as a foil. I also learned to situate myself so I would shine—whether it be in the reflection of the sun or the bright lights on State Street.

Suzy and I had always lived in the same neighborhood and were used to dating boys we had grown up with. It was thrilling and liberating to realize those sailors knew nothing at all about us. They didn't know we had sneaked out of a performance of *The Sound of Music* to try to entice them. They didn't know that when we weren't walking the street, we were studying so we could get into a good college. Best of all, they didn't know our parents, which meant they wouldn't tell them what we were up to.

There was something about this anonymity that made my heart pound under my cashmere sweater set. I wouldn't have that feeling again for twenty years, until I started traveling the world alone and meeting men who were similarly disconnected from my life back home.

But when Suzy and I were fifteen, the sailors on State Street were our only contact with the outside world. They represented adventure and danger. With their muscles bulging under their crisp uniforms, they were masculine in a way that made the boys we were going out with look like twerps. Once we had a sailor's attention, though, we didn't know what to do with it. We would run away if one came too close. If he pursued us, we would act outraged, as if there had been a terrible misunderstanding.

On a few occasions, we actually spoke to the sailors. They didn't talk as well as they looked. Usually, they were from a small town and homesick. Looking back, they must have found us with our big-city airs a little intimidating. But that would not have occurred to Suzy or me. We hadn't yet developed a sensitivity to what boys might be feeling. Anyway, they weren't boys. They were sailors.

Same Old Thing at a Singles Party

I am applying Extra Red lipstick with a brush, stretching my mouth in the mirror in a vain attempt to paint perfect curves. On either side of me, women are putting on translucent powder, blush, eyeliner and mascara—all with the same single-minded zeal. The ladies' room in the bar of a downtown office building reeks of perfumes, a combined fragrance that could be bottled under the name Anticipation.

We are engaged in a familiar ritual known as Getting Ourselves Ready to Meet Men. If I half close my eyes, I can imagine myself back in the girls' room at Lake View High School, stuffing Kleenex in my bra in the hope that the boys at the mixer will notice me. But I am no longer fourteen, and, as I head toward the bar where a singles party is in full swing, I think to myself, I am getting too old for this.

That's the problem I have with singles events of any kind. Once you reach a certain point in life, you shouldn't have strangers passing judgment on you—and not really even on you, but on your looks and whether you are their type. It's uncomfortable to be sized up like a slave at auction, and undignified. Of course, singles are always eyeing each other; but formalizing the process and calling it a party is not my idea of fun.

So what am I doing at a singles function on a Friday night when I could be at the movies? I have come because I realize that, for many people, these parties are the best chance of connecting and because this particular one has a gimmick that does sound like fun.

The invitation requested that we bring along a personals ad

describing ourselves and what we're looking for in another person. The idea is that we hand them out at the party, thereby saving ourselves a lot of explaining.

For those who arrive ad-less—either out of forgetfulness or, in my case, because we don't know what to say—a writer with experience at this sort of thing is available to compose one for us. I'm fascinated by how he can take complicated thoughts and compress them into a word or two. After telling him I love the theater, symphony and ballet, the noun he uses to capture me is "culture vulture."

My saying I want someone who exercises and watches his diet, but not in an obnoxious way, translates simply as "fit." However, I think my Boswell went too far when he wrote that I'm interested in "aural sex"—because I told him I'm partial to men who can talk and also listen.

Some of the ads people have come up with themselves are quite clever. One woman reproduced a group office snapshot, identified herself, and added a postscript that should you be interested in anyone else in the picture: "I do charge a fee." A man listed his likes, including Dartmouth hockey games and hot air balloons, and such dislikes as asbestos and slugs "or anything slimy."

However, armed with my own advertisement, I quickly discover the fallacy of a personals party. Confronted with the actual person, nobody pays any attention to the ads. Why read about someone when you can check him or her out yourself?

So it turns out to be just another singles party, with people's eyeballs darting around so fast they appear to be unhinged. I notice one man who seems to be going out of his way to walk by me. Our eyes meet, and he raises his eyebrows. Is this some kind of secret sign known only to frequent singles party-goers? I laugh. That must not be the correct response, since he disappears back into the crowd.

Another guy walks up to me—for some reason, women do not come up to men at singles parties—and starts talking. I know what an act of courage this is and I am determined to be nice to him, even though he really isn't my type. He asks what I am currently reading, a perfectly legitimate question except I have the feeling it is on some kind of list of good opening lines. I tell him *Lolita*, and immediately regret having said that. It sounds too provocative.

I excuse myself and make a beeline for the buffet table. I note that half the party is congregated there. It's a safe haven. With your mouth full, you have a perfect excuse not to talk to anyone. And if you're having a terrible time, you can always rationalize that you just came for the food.

I go back to the bathroom, another safe haven. A woman who has just arrived is asking a veteran if the party is worth going to. The second woman ponders the question.

"It depends on what you want," she finally says. I agree with her. What I want is to get out of there.

Power Matchmaking
D.C.-Style

What kind of singles party would a United States Senator throw? That question intrigued me enough to fly across the country to attend a fabled gathering sponsored by Minnesota Senator Rudy Boschwitz—otherwise known as the Matchmaker of Capitol Hill. His parties have a reputation for being where you go when you tire of playing around and want to settle down.

The Republican senator started giving them five years ago in response to complaints from staff members that it was impossible to meet anyone in Washington. In his office he keeps "trophies"— the dozens of wedding and birth announcements sent to him by couples who met at his functions.

Parents and grandparents write to Boschwitz (happily married for thirty-three years), begging him to work his matchmaking magic on their single offspring. He makes sure they are invited to his next party. The senator acknowledges a special interest in Jewish singles and is doing his part to bring them together.

I'm not sure what I expected, but walking into the party I was struck by how much it resembled every other singles event—the same palpable nervousness, the same sizing each other up like a slave at auction, the same anonymous room with chairs lined up along the side in anticipation of wallflowers, even the same boring hors d'oeuvres.

People would walk in, look around and appear as if they were going to bolt. That was easy to do at this party, which came with a money-back guarantee. If you left within fifteen minutes, the $12 entrance fee was refunded in full.

Although marriage wasn't on my agenda, knowing how elite the bash was supposed to be, I was determined to make an impression. As the song says, "If I can make it there, I'll make it anywhere."

I wore a sleek, leopard-print dress that stood out among the frilly pastels. (The invitation had said semi-formal, whatever that means.) While other women traveled in packs—always a mistake, since a guy would have to be pretty self-confident or drunk to try to break in—I stood alone in the center of the room scribbling in a note pad. This provides men with an obvious opening line: "What are you writing?" I recommend a notebook even to women who have no reason to take notes.

Sure enough, men came to me. It was only then that I realized how young they were. They all seemed to be twenty-seven, which shouldn't have been so surprising. That's the age when you think about getting married, at least for the first time. I felt like Mrs. Robinson in *The Graduate* flirting back when my twenty-seven-year-olds said they couldn't believe I was past forty, that I didn't look a day over thirty-five and that age didn't matter, anyway.

I wasn't the only one in the crowded room to be hustled. There was a lot of deep eye contact going on and phone numbers hastily being written on party napkins. There was also the usual deception. A hyper lawyer had just finished telling me she asks men for their numbers to get rid of them, when I ran into one of her rejects. The poor fellow said that as far as he was concerned the party was a success because a woman he really liked had promised to call.

As the band played the last song, people made plans to leave with someone other than the person with whom they had come. One woman with Farrah Fawcett–type hair seemed to be rubbing it in by parading her catch in front of her plain girlfriend, who agreed to drive the blonde's car home for her.

One of my twenty-seven-year-olds—I'll call him Sonny—offered me a ride. He worked on Capitol Hill, so I figured he wasn't Jack the Ripper. Besides, he seemed so sweet. I mentioned I had a pretty twenty-two-year-old niece I wished he could meet. Sonny said he thought I was pretty. He turned his head, and I noticed him spray his mouth with breath freshener. He asked whether I believed you should go with your feelings. I said absolutely, that people lose out by playing it safe. When we got to my hotel, Sonny pulled over and said he was glad I felt that way because he had this incredible urge to kiss me.

I was dumbstruck (that happens when you're as dumb as I am). It suddenly dawned on me the breath freshener had been for my benefit. I thought about the earnest senator and how this couldn't possibly be what he had in mind. And then I laughed in Sonny's face, though really in the face of all grandiose attempts at matchmaking.

Dialing for a Chance at Romance

Mike and I are talking marriage, not to each other—it's a little soon for that—but in general. He says he definitely would like to get married and that he came awfully close with his last girlfriend. Something in his tone makes me wonder if their relationship is as over and done with as he is leading me to believe.

This is the stuff of first-date conversations, except that Mike and I have never laid eyes on one another, nor is it likely we ever will. We have only met over the telephone, on one of those recreational party lines you hear advertised on late-night TV as the latest way for singles to connect.

That's not false advertising if it's quantity you're after. I hooked up with an awful lot of men the Saturday night I spent dialing for romance. There was marriageable Mike from Colorado, Jack from Virginia, Sid from Pennsylvania, Steve from Connecticut, Chris from Oregon, Frank from South Carolina, and a bunch of other guys I didn't talk to long enough to exchange names and states.

The geographical spread surprised me, since the party lines I called were exclusively in San Francisco and Los Angeles. I hadn't realized so many men all over the country have fantasies about wild and crazy California girls that these lines are allowing them to indulge.

As soon as I said hello, a chorus of male voices began pleading with me to call them at home collect. They couldn't wait to get me alone. And I hadn't even said where I was from yet. (The male-female ratio on party lines is about five-to-one, so there is stiff competition to make a phone date fast.) I had beginner's luck, getting Mike on the other end my first time. I liked his voice; it sounded comforting.

As I later learned, guys who call party lines can be divided into two categories: those who want to get to know you first and those who are interested in only one thing. Mike was in the former group. When I phoned him back, he made it seem as if he had nothing to do except chat (which may actually have been the case). He asked me about my hobbies and my favorite movies. His ploy to find out what I look like was offering to guess—and then flattering me wildly with his description. I had the feeling he'd done this before.

Jack, on the other hand, had no time for small talk. He let me know he was a busy man by informing me he had just come back from a business trip to the West Coast. When I asked what he did for a living, he became impatient.

"You know most people who call up party lines are frankly just interested in phone sex," he said.

That seemed a good time to tell him I worked for a newspaper. If that was so, he retorted indignantly, right before hanging up, why was he paying for the call?

My phone encounters have helped me understand the phenomenon of party lines. They are incredibly popular, with some callers spending hundreds of dollars a month on them. (The service costs $1 a minute, in addition to whatever long-distance charges are incurred. Jack told me men always offer to let the women call them collect, never the other way around, "because women don't like to run up huge phone bills.")

For the AIDS generation, party lines are the ultimate in safe sex. I suspect people may be getting a thrill similar to what they used to get at singles bars. You can say anything you want to this total stranger and be as seductive or roguish as you always knew you were.

A phone is even better for this kind of acting out than a bar. It's easier to sound sexy than to look it. And if things get out of hand, you can always hang up: the quickest way to just say no. But for me the only value of a party line is if it leads to a face-to-face meeting (not that I'm advocating it as a way to meet). I'm trying hard not to make moral judgments, but I find it weird that the guys I talked to could be satisfied with just phone talk, with or without heavy breathing. It seems so isolating. If that's your idea of fun, don't call me. And don't hold your breath waiting for me to call you, either.

A Date's No Buddy's Business

Not long after my divorce, a friend called to say she had found the perfect man for me. He was a doctor, involved in some kind of lifesaving research. She reeled off his attributes like a determined auctioneer. I told her I hated to be fixed up, but she would hear none of it. The match was as good as struck.

Sure enough, a few days later Dr. Right appeared at my doorstep. He said, "Hello." I said "Hello." The next words were a real struggle for both of us.

I didn't like his looks, his voice, his laugh or the way he looked past me when I was talking. Perhaps he was looking for the door. It was rather obvious he didn't think I was so hot either. The things we had in common were that we were both single and breathing. Was that what my friend had meant by the perfect man for me?

That was the last time I allowed myself to be matched up. Finding someone you want to go out with is so personal. I wouldn't send my friends to pick out lingerie for me. Why should I trust them to pick out men? I see it as the difference between ordering from a catalog and doing your own shopping. You can read all about a product, but you don't really know what you're getting until you've inspected the merchandise. Matchmaking is a risky business. When the date your closest friend has arranged for you turns out to be a dud, it's hard not to wonder: "What is it about me that made my friend think I'd be interested in this turkey?"

I should get a dubious distinction award for the matchmaking I've done. Two couples I had fixed up got engaged, then disengaged under ugly circumstances. In one case, the woman refused to give back the diamond ring, and her ex-fiancé had to wrest it off her finger.

My friend Patti has the best track record as a matchmaker of anyone I know. Eight marriages have resulted from her efforts. She doesn't consider it her fault that at least seven of the couples have divorced. She's lost track of the eighth.

Some might argue that at least you know what you're getting with a fix-up, that a person handpicked by your friends comes with some kind of seal of approval. All I have to say is that, in 1924, a mutual friend arranged for my mother to go out with Richard Loeb. A few months later, he and his buddy, Nathan Leopold, killed a fourteen-year-old boy in cold blood—a murder story that shocked all Chicagoans, especially my mother, who thought Richard seemed like such a nice young man.

Another Woman Who Got Away

Three women walked into the hall together right ahead of us. With the eye of a professional photographer and experienced ladies man, Mark checked them out and decided he had to meet the one on the right in navy-and-white polka dots.

It was a delicate situation. There were the feelings of her companions to consider. *My* feelings were not an issue. Mark and I are, as they say, just friends. I could almost hear his mind clicking, like the shutter on a camera, as he tried to come up with an opening line fast.

"I noticed each of you is wearing a different size heel, and I was curious which was more comfortable," Mark blurted out.

Not a great line, but it did the job of including the three women while clearly being directed at just one. The woman in polka dots laughed and kept on walking. Click, click, went her heels.

Mark had a hard time concentrating on the ballet, which was what we had come for. He was obsessed with finding her again. Several times I caught him peering through his opera glasses at the audience instead of the stage. During intermission and after the performance, he continued his search. But the polka dots he spotted all turned out to be on the wrong body.

Mark blamed me for losing her. I had split the moment he made his move. After years of hanging out with him, I'm used to getting out of the way. However, in Mark's opinion, I hadn't been quick enough this time. He was certain the woman in polka dots had seen me and deduced we were a couple.

"It's a funny thing about women. They'll never show any interest in a man if he's with someone," he said. That didn't strike me as funny; it struck me as virtuous.

Mark believes a lot of women would like to respond to moves made on them, but worry to do so would be improper. They are so concerned with how it might look that they let the moment pass and the man get away.

(Before he complains some more, let me add his efforts have sometimes been rewarded. He had a brief romance with a woman who passed him on the freeway. She was on a motorcycle with a guitar hanging over her back. Mark caught up with her and held a note out the window, which he had hastily composed. It said: "Dinner?")

Mark is also annoyed with women for almost never making the first move.

"It's not their nature to be the aggressor, which is fine except they shouldn't be so hard on us for trying," he said.

He has a point. I have to admit I usually ignore men I don't know when they talk to me. I don't consider what an effort it might be on their part to say anything.

For instance, once when I was out running, a male jogger suddenly appeared at my side and said, "Nice day for a run." I had a feeling he wasn't interested only in the weather. But it didn't seem appropriate to respond. Like the woman in polka dots, I walked—or, rather, ran—on by.

I'm quite sure I have never approached a stranger and said something solely to get him to notice me. I did once go out with a Belgian I had stopped on a street in Brussels to ask for directions; the difference was I honestly wanted directions.

My style, if I'm attracted to someone, is to find out who he is and write him a note. (This implies I have a way of tracking him down, which eliminates chance encounters in public places.) I can be endlessly brave and charming in writing.

Mark and I are alike in that we're both fatalists when it comes to encounters like these. I have often heard him say, "If it's meant to be, it will happen." However, in the case of the encounter at the ballet, I'm willing to give fate a nudge.

So, woman in polka dots, if you happen to be reading this and recognize yourself or your wardrobe, call me. I have this really nice friend who would still like to meet you.

Missing Out on Being the Chosen One

It was such a silly thing, really, that, with everything else I have to worry about, I don't know why I let it bother me.

I had gone over to my neighborhood café to sip a cappuccino and stare into space. I was just settling in when a woman carrying a stack of papers in one hand and a coffee cup in the other asked if I would mind if she joined me.

As a matter of fact, I did mind. I wanted to be alone, which I prefer to do surrounded, though not too closely, by other people. But there weren't any empty tables, and I couldn't very well just let her stand there. She immediately busied herself with her papers, and I felt reassured that she was only looking for a seat and not a new friend.

A few minutes later, I was conscious of a male voice breaking the silence. The guy next to us was asking my table mate what she was studying so hard and various other questions meant to convey his interest in her.

My first reaction was annoyance similar to what I'd felt when, after waiting more than an hour at a restaurant, my husband at the time and I were seated with two men who spent the entire meal hustling a pair of unaccompanied women next to them. If I'd wanted to hear that, I would have gone to a singles bar. Then it occurred to me that, since I had no husband with me this time, the man at the next table could just as well be cozying up to me. For reasons known only to him, he had chosen the other woman.

I took a critical look at her. She was one of those pale blondes who was a knockout in high school, but was not aging particularly well. She already had more wrinkles than I do, though I guessed her to be at least ten years younger.

I was startled to hear him ask if she might be a journalist. (I don't understand what had led him to the question, since her papers had math tables all over them.) She was not, she said. I had to stop myself from piping in, "But I am," which would have been tantamount to shouting, "Look at me."

Understand, I was not the slightest bit interested in this man. He wasn't my type any more than I apparently was his. If he had come on to me, I would have been even cooler than the faded blonde. I just wanted to be the rejecter and not the rejectee.

The experience brought back memories of being on the sidelines at a mixer and having the guy who seemed to be headed your way veer to the left at the last moment and talk to another woman. Everyone wants to be the chosen one, if for no other reason than that the alternative is too humiliating.

I'm sure I have been chosen more often than not. Yet it is the times I have been ignored—including when I went to the Cajun country with my friend Sylvia and three men at a local bar asked her to dance and nobody asked me—that I tend to remember. Of course, one can always rationalize these things. Sylvia is a wonderful dancer so it was logical that after her first spin around the floor, other men would rush to her side.

The friend I used to go boy hunting with in high school was barely five feet tall. The times she was chosen over me, I could rationalize that the fellow must like his girls short.

When I was newly single, I made the rounds of meeting places with a blond girlfriend. The gentlemen who looked at her rather than at me, I surmised, preferred blondes. (There was one guy from Sweden who was interested in both of us; after we explained we weren't a package deal, he lost interest entirely.)

It could be that the man at the café also preferred blondes, or that he liked younger women or that this woman so dazzled him he never saw me at all. Or it could be that my attire—running shorts and a T-shirt—put him off, though the same outfit has drawn appreciative glances from other men.

In a perfect world, there would be a man for every woman (preferably, the one she wanted), and women's egos would not so easily be bruised. But as we know too well, it doesn't work that way. That's why I think you should do your serious looking by yourself. It's bad enough to find yourself competing with a stranger in a café. Who needs to do it with a friend?

WHAT ARE YOU LOOKING FOR?

A lot of us are out there looking without really knowing what we're looking for. We vacillate wildly. Those scary studies about how we have almost no chance of ever finding a mate lead us to believe anybody is better than nobody. Going to a wedding can also make you willing to settle for anyone who can make it down the aisle. However, faced with a warm body, we become incredibly picky and decide he or she does not measure up to our favorite movie stars.

It's a mistake to be wedded to an ideal image. Each person deserves to be judged on his or her merits. Still, there are certain things that would knock someone out of the running. Married people are not date material. Neither is someone of a different faith or political persuasion, if those things are important to you.

The Man Glut: A Word About Quality

I was not one of those single women who panicked when the by-now notorious Harvard–Yale study came out in 1986. I read that women my age with my educational background had almost no chance of ever finding anyone to marry—we have a better chance of being killed by a terrorist, in the immortal words of *Newsweek*—and I decided I wasn't going to worry about it.

I have a perhaps foolhardy belief that anything I really want, I can make happen. Following that logic, if you can, I'm not married because deep down I don't want to be. The man shortage is irrelevant. Also, I cling to the romantic notion that there's somebody for everyone. Statistical analyses are antithetical to such a notion. The lyricist who wrote "Someday my prince will come. . ." wasn't referring to population projections. What's made me think about this again is new news from the bearer of the original bad news.

Now Neil Bennett, the Yale sociologist responsible for the gloom-and-doom study, says there is about to be an abundance of available men, and fewer women will be frustrated in their efforts to marry. However, before you start shopping for your trousseau, you should know this shift in the male-to-female ratio applies only to those in their twenties and younger.

Before anyone buys anything frilly, I think we should all seriously question what ratios have to do with affairs of the heart. After all, it's not as if all single people had been invited to the same mixer, and you could see the disparity between the sexes spread out before you. Imagine millions of women over thirty-five as wallflowers. Not a pretty sight.

Fortunately, in real life, nobody has to stand on the sidelines. You can increase your chances of meeting someone simply by going where members of the opposite sex are likely to be. I figured that out when I was eleven and enrolled in Bar Mitzvah class. I was one of two girls in a room of twenty-seven, making the boy-to-girl ratio 100 to 7.4. Take that, Mr. Bennett.

While sociologists concern themselves with quantity, I'd like to say a few words on behalf of quality.

I may have been born at the wrong time and moved to the wrong city (everybody knows there aren't any men in San Francisco), but meeting men has never been a problem for me. Finding one I would like to spend an evening with, let alone the rest of my life—that's the hard part. Like the Marines, women with any sense are looking for "a few good men." An increase in the male population is no guarantee of an increase in quality.

This isn't the first time there's been a dearth of available men. What nature's quirks haven't made uneven, world wars have. But this is the first time the shortage has touched off a panic among women. It's been reflected in all those books and movies that tell us what we're doing wrong and that we better get married before it's too late.

The reason past generations of women haven't despaired is that they've had families and a social structure to help them find a man. It wasn't so long ago that arranged marriages were the norm and this thing called love an aberration. Now so many of us live adrift. We have to fend for ourselves. When that gets rough, as it invariably does, we're eager to find someone or something to blame.

Along with anger, I detected relief when the first study came out, as if it absolved women of wrongdoing. It wasn't their fault they hadn't met anyone; there wasn't anyone to meet. It will be interesting to see how another, younger generation responds to the new population research. Will men panic? Will women gloat? Or will singles finally realize *they* control their destiny— not the experts?

Mr. Ideal Is Revealed in Little Ways

I just read another study in which women describe what they're looking for in a man. Mr. Ideal, reports *Psychology Today*, is wise, compassionate, spiritual, self-actualized and not afraid of intimacy—sort of a cross between Alan Alda and Mahatma Gandhi.

I have no quarrel with any of these qualities, though I suspect a man who possessed all of them would be something else as well: insufferable. But I don't get the point of studies such as this one, unless it's to make women feel bad about the lout they wound up with. Having a mental picture of how your ideal is supposed to look and act is only setting yourself up to be disappointed.

You can't custom-order a mate like you can a fancy sports car. He or she will already have been assembled when you meet, complete with options you may not want. You have to decide whether you can live with the package. At the same time, Mr. or Ms. Less-Than-Ideal will be making the same decision about you. (A peculiarity of the dating ritual is that people rarely seem aware that they are being judged even as they are judging.)

I'm tired of hearing girlfriends say, "So-and-so isn't my type," especially since they're never able to describe exactly what their type is. They have a gauzy image of Kevin Costner in mind and use it as an excuse not to give so-and-so a chance.

The men I've gone out with have been a disparate-looking lot. About the only thing they have in common is that they've all towered over me. Had I been rigid about Really Tall being my type, I would never have met the shorter man who made me realize height doesn't matter. A person's character, however, can't be given short shrift. It does matter. But character takes a long time to unfold. Meanwhile, it's the little things that make you fall for someone—or never want to see him or her again.

For instance, I found it endearing when, on our first date, I turned around unexpectedly and caught Frank combing his hair. He immediately became embarrassed because, of course, he was combing it for me, and he knew I knew that. The sight of this terribly distinguished older man blushing like a teenager made me want to hug him. He turned out to have many more endearing qualities.

On the other hand, I knew it was never going to work between Joel and me when on our third date he told me about his trip to Spain for the third time, using exactly the same words. I had to restrain myself from finishing his sentences.

I'm the worst person to repeat a story to. I have a reporter's memory and never forget anything anyone tells me. Still, I had to wonder about Joel's limited repertoire. Surely in forty-five years he'd had more than one interesting experience.

A sense of humor invariably ranks high on a checklist of desirable traits. But I've found just having a sense of humor alone isn't enough; it needs to dovetail with mine.

Despite what happened the only time we went out, I don't believe Stan is humorless. Dense, maybe, but not humorless. He just takes himself too seriously to be a good match for me. I knew he had a lot of money and was into conspicuous consumption. So when we were walking to his car and I noticed him slowing down near a beat-up jalopy parked by a cream-colored Lamborghini, I couldn't resist pointing to the jalopy and asking, "Is that yours?"

I was astonished when Stan answered with a hurt "No."

There didn't seem much point in explaining I was only kidding. I simply got into the Lamborghini and kept my jokes to myself during what turned into a very long evening.

A study of the perfect man has yet to be devised with categories for "Blushes Like a Teenager" or "Doesn't Bore Me to Distraction" or "Appreciates My Weird Sense of Humor." But these little things mean a lot. Taken together, they act like windows into someone's character—though you have to be pretty wise to see how.

Dreaming of Doing Things Frank's Way

I've been having sexy dreams about Frank Sinatra. I only remember one of them, which is embarrassing enough, but even as it was unfolding I had a feeling—the French would call it *déjà rêvé*—I'd had this dream before.

I am pursuing Sinatra in the hope of getting an interview. I know this will not be easy, given his disdain for the press, but I am persistent. I track him down to a small, elegant hotel and camp outside his door. He arrives with none of the bodyguards I'd expected. I giggle and flutter my eyelashes and do all the things women do to get their way. Amazingly, it works. Sinatra invites me in.

I start to fire questions at him, but he gently takes my reporter's notebook out of my hand and replaces it with his hand. I notice how blue his eyes are. We embrace.

The next thing I remember (well actually I do remember some of what happens in between, but, as I said, this is embarrassing) is that we are sitting around his suite in silk dressing gowns, like the ones I imagine Sinatra wears when he is not in a tuxedo. A butler is serving us dinner (champagne and caviar, followed by steak and potatoes), after which he discreetly disappears, and I have Frank to myself for the rest of the dream.

Sinatra has been on my mind lately, so it is not totally improbable that he should pop up in my dreams. I've been listening to a lot of his old albums. Even with my stereo off, I can still hear him crooning, "You Go to My Head" and "I've Got You Under My Skin."

I also just saw the re-release of *The Manchurian Candidate*, in which Sinatra plays a guy obsessed with a recurrent dream. That could be where my unconscious got the idea; though I suspect it has more to do with how sexy Sinatra was in that movie. It was made in 1962, when he was forty-six and still had that lean and hungry look. Every woman in the audience understands why Janet Leigh would make a pass at him, even if he was a stranger in the night. The Sinatra of my dreams looks like he did back then.

The dream was a kind of wish fulfillment, but only in the sense that I would love to interview him—even if he has called women journalists "broads and buck-and-a-half hookers." Later, Sinatra apologized to hookers for the comparison: "Newswomen sell their souls," he said. "Who would want their bodies?" So, maybe I was just trying to show him he was wrong about us.

No self-respecting shrink would let me get away with such a superficial analysis. I can practically hear one saying, with a Viennese accent, of course, "Ah, yes, but what's the real reason you are having sex dreams about Frank Sinatra?"

They should make me wonder if I secretly long for the type of man Sinatra represents: the kind who calls women "broads" and is fully capable of roughing them up, even if he doesn't actually do so. I've certainly never been attracted to that type; I like my men sensitive and literate.

Yet I have to admit there is something appealing about a "dangerous man," especially one with all the power Sinatra commands. I could be another of his lackeys, kept around only as long as I please the master, but so *well* kept that I do everything I can not to fall out of favor. I would have to give up my job, since, as I recall, Sinatra has never wanted his women to work. That was one reason his marriage to Mia Farrow broke up. I'd just stay home, take bubble baths and have my toenails painted.

At last, Dr. Freud, it is coming to me: the meaning of the dream. I do not get what I thought I wanted—namely, an interview—but maybe Sinatra knows better what women really want. The notebook does not reappear after he takes it away, and I ask no more questions. In the end, he does it his way.

Dad, I Can't Get You Out of My Life

I have always been uneasy around Father's Day, probably because I was always uneasy around my father. He kindled so many different emotions in me—from awe to anger to exasperation—that fifteen years after his death I still find it hard to talk about him. Today, I suppose he would be called an entrepreneur. I wish that word had been around when I was trying to think of something to put under "Father's occupation" and envying my classmates who had a simple answer.

My father was in the shoe business, the clothing business, the nightclub business, the restaurant business and the boxing business. And those are just the occupations I *know* about. Boxing was where he came the closest to making it big. He turned down a chance to handle Joe Louis—family legend has it that Louis lost the night Dad went to check him out—and ended up managing a bunch of boxers who could have been contenders, but weren't. He also promoted some major fights in Chicago, but was edged out when the sport began to be televised.

Still, my father made a lot of money in his heyday. He spent even more. One of my earliest memories is watching him take out a wad of one-hundred-dollar bills and peeling them off as if they were singles.

My mother, on the other hand, was an eminently practical woman. After she tired of his extravagance and left him, he became this dashing figure who flitted in and out of my life. For months, I would keep track of him by the insurance policies that arrived from airports all over the country. Then he would reappear and swoop me up in an existence that was right out of the movies. He was handsome in a Cary Grant way and perennially tan. He dressed in silk shirts, custom-made three-piece suits and hats with brims that were pulled down just so. (His taste in clothes leaned toward the flamboyant. A boxing writer I know tells me that in New York fight circles, my dad was known for his chartreuse pants.)

He was more like an Uncle Mame than a father. He took me to fancy restaurants and told me to order anything I wanted, and didn't get upset when I couldn't finish a third of it. When I was ten, I went with him to the Chez Paree, then the hot Chicago nightclub, to see Zsa Zsa Gabor. After the show, Dad introduced me to her. They seemed to be old pals.

For a Bar Mitzvah party, he bought me a $100 blue satin gown with a bouffant skirt. It was hardly appropriate for a twelve-year-old, but I loved it. I cried when it came back from the cleaners with all the puff taken out.

My feelings toward him changed by the time I became a teenager. I sided with my mother in whatever had transpired between them, though I wouldn't understand it for years. I stopped returning his calls and, when he sought me out, I literally ran from him. But I could never get completely away. I kept reading about him in the newspapers. Newspapermen courted my father, and now that I'm in the business, I understand why. He made lively copy. Even after he died, he continued to be a presence.

He has had an enormous influence over my choice of men. I didn't marry my father, nor have I gone out with anyone vaguely like him. If a man takes longer than one sentence to explain what he does for a living, I start looking for the nearest exit. The men I have been serious about have all been professionals: doctors, lawyers or college professors. They have been stable and reliable and about as flamboyant as George Bush. They wouldn't dream of wearing bright-colored slacks, except to play golf—the kind of gentlemen's sport my father never understood.

But I no longer want to totally negate my father, assuming that I could. I have come to terms with the fact that he was not like other people's dads. It has taken me forty-four Father's Days to finally recognize the gifts he gave me that are even better than a satin gown, because they are mine for keeps. In his own way, he made me feel special, and he made me feel loved.

When He's Younger, It's Trouble

It's hard to pick up a magazine without reading about how happy Cher is with one or another of her young boyfriends. The twenty-year-or-so age difference between her and these men is no big deal, or so she keeps saying. She and one of her honeys even joked about it. He took her face in his hands and squished it up to see what she will look like when she's old and wrinkled (though with her plastic surgeon, surely it will never come to that).

It may be easy for Cher, but I wonder if it's such a cinch for other women in their forties to go out with men young enough to be their sons. There's a lot of conditioning to be overcome first. I know how women of that generation were brought up, since I'm one of them. Our idea of the perfect date with someone who was older and taller than us. We wanted to be able to look up to our men.

Come to think of it, Cher also broke the height barrier. She towered over Sonny. Remember what an odd couple they made on TV?

Even though the rules have changed and it is now fashionable to have a young boyfriend, I have a sense women still feel something is not quite right about such an arrangement. The only younger man I've ever had a serious relationship with was a mere eight years my junior. Yet the age difference affected everything between us. I felt as if I knew more than he did because I had been around longer, and I couldn't resist making him the beneficiary of my supposed knowledge. At first, he was receptive; later, he became annoyed.

I have gone out with men ten and fifteen years older than I am and never thought about age. But when I was with my young man, I couldn't not think about it. It was a pervasive issue and, ultimately, a destructive one.

A friend of mine used to live with a man fifteen years

younger. She told me when they would go to parties, she would look at women his age and think he should be going out with one of them. Then, of course, she would become jealous if he so much as glanced their way. It was a no-win situation—which was why she finally got out of it.

I'm not saying these relationships can never work. I'm just saying they're not as simple as they look in *People* magazine.

Cher is used to being stared at. She wouldn't know anymore if it was for her belly button or her boyfriend. But most women in May/December romances are not accustomed to that kind of attention. They become incredibly self-conscious, mortified at the thought that they might be mistaken for their date's mother. One woman I know usually ends up cooking dinner for her young boyfriend. It fulfills her maternal instincts, and she has found it's easier to stay home than deal with the looks they invariably get dining out.

Older men have had more experience at this sort of thing. I imagine a man in his fifties would welcome being stared at in the company of a woman in her twenties. It would make him feel like he was quite a guy. Men also are realistic about their allure. They understand it has more to do with whatever money or power or fame they may have acquired than with love.

When women are the ones who are older, however, they still cling to their romantic notions. They don't want to see their relationship as a business deal—even if they are supporting the guy or have to pay him $180,000 to get rid of him (as Joan Collins did as part of her divorce settlement). The more a woman has at stake emotionally, the greater the risk she will end up feeling foolish. Of course, there's always that risk any time you let yourself feel for someone. But somehow it seems worse for a woman to be making a fool of herself over a young man.

Lena Horne really hit that nerve when she introduced the song "Bewitched" during her Broadway show as the story of an "old broad with money who falls in love with a young, young stud." The old broad's problem wasn't that she bedded down with this man, but that she allowed herself to be bewitched, bothered and bewildered by him. That's the way women tend to respond. We're funny that way. Cher's love life notwithstanding, it becomes more complicated, not easier, as we get older and the men get younger.

The Perfect Man Has a Wife and Kids

Nora didn't wait for me to say hello before she started talking. Her voice, even over the phone, sounded electric. She had either found a great bargain or a man, and I was right to suspect the latter. They had met, Nora was saying, when she went to his law office to see about suing those painters who had wrecked the exterior of her house. It was funny how she had put on her new spring suit—the one with the very short skirt—as if she had had a premonition this was going to happen.

All the lawyer had done was introduce himself, and already she felt like the ground had been pulled out from under her. It wasn't just that he was impossibly cute, with Paul Newman— blue eyes and hair more shades of gray than a fog bank. There was chemistry between them, and maybe even physics.

Nora kept talking. I was superfluous to our conversation. She should have been asking him all sorts of legal questions, but all she had really wanted to know was if he was married. Then she spotted the obligatory family photos on the wall. Of course, there was a wife in the picture. Nora had sort of known there would be. She also knew the flirtation should have ended right there. But, sitting across from him, staring into those eyes, she hadn't been able to stop herself from giggling, as if the prospect of a lawsuit against one's house painters were terribly amusing.

The lawyer had suddenly gotten up and moved his chair next to her. She could smell him and, by shifting slightly, she could have touched him. And she knew if she did that, she would be irretrievably lost.

She told him about a trip she was planning to France. The

subject wasn't as off the wall as it sounded, she said, answering my question without giving me a chance to ask it. If she did decide to go ahead with the suit, the lawyer should know she would be away for several weeks. "You going alone?" he asked, except it came out sounding more like an order than a question. Before she could answer, he was saying he would love to go back to France, where he had spent his junior year in college.

That was all Nora needed to hear. In the few days since they had met, she had all but booked a trip for them. She imagined them bicycling through Normandy and having intimate conversations over *café au lait* at the Deux Magots on the Left Bank. His wife was definitely not in the picture.

Nora told me he was in her thoughts all the time. She was waking up early thinking about him. He was affecting her work and her life, and she really didn't know what to do about it.

You don't have to have seen *Fatal Attraction* or have read *Presumed Innocent* to know she should get herself another lawyer. Any rational person, which Nora was not at the moment, must realize that affairs with married people are always tawdry and inevitably end badly. But you can't say that to someone who is in the throes of it. She thought she was in love with the guy. Who was I to remind her that she didn't even know him or to suggest that probably what she was in love with was how illicit it all seemed?

To rationalize seeing him again, Nora was telling herself all those things that sound like lines from Barry Manilow songs. You only go around once. How could anything bad feel so good? A few stolen days with him would be better than a lifetime with somebody else. And, lastly, she asked the big question: Is there a God and does he care?

At that moment of decision, does anyone really think about the betrayed spouse or the children who could be hurt in ways they won't understand for years? I doubt it. You're too busy fantasizing sex the way you never knew it could be. I know how tempting that is—and how pointless it would have been for me or any of Nora's other friends to recommend self-control. She was so far gone that not even a shopping spree would have helped her forget him.

Nora called me again a week after our first conversation. The lawyer wanted to have lunch with her. He said he had some ideas about how she could avoid a lawsuit and still get her house fixed. She wanted to know if I thought it would be possible for them to just have lunch. I told her what she must have known: that if they got together again, it would be for more than lunch.

What should she do? Nora asked plaintively. I didn't answer. She wouldn't have listened anyway.

The Politics of the Heart Run Deep

While playing at a girlfriend's house one day in 1956, I noticed "I Like Ike" buttons strewn all over the hall credenza. The conclusion I reluctantly came to was confirmed by my friend: Her parents were Republicans. I was shocked, not only because they were the first Republicans I had ever known, but because they were perfectly nice—not at all the fuddy-duddies I had imagined people of that political persuasion to be.

I have since gotten to know many more Republicans and discovered that niceness is not correlated with party affiliation. Part of growing up is realizing you are not always going to like everyone who agrees with you, or dislike everyone who doesn't. However, I can't recall ever having gone out with a Republican, and I know I have never had a relationship with one. The closest I came was a brief fling with a Libertarian.

It's not as if I make a point of turning down dates from Republicans, but that I rarely meet any in a social context. I don't run in Republican circles and never have. I was brought up Jewish and Democratic—not necessarily in that order. My mother would bundle up on chilly Chicago nights to canvass for her hero, Adlai Stevenson. Studs Terkel lived down the street from us, so I got to hear him, in person as well as on the radio, espouse what would now be called old-fashioned liberal ideas.

Some of my friends' parents were rich, but their money was so new they had yet to develop the reflex to protect it that turns some people into Republicans. They spent it on lavish Bar Mitzvahs for their sons and Sweet Sixteen parties for their little princesses. But their sympathies were with those who had less (perhaps because they could still remember what that was like), and when they voted, it was Democratic.

My first real exposure to Republicans was at Northwestern University in the early 1960s. Everybody on campus except me and a handful of friends seemed to be Young Republicans.

The guys were business majors before it was chic. They didn't care about grades, since they knew they would be taking over their daddies' companies. In fact, they didn't seem to care about much except their fraternity and which pretty coed they would be going out with Saturday night.

I was not one of the coeds they called, so this could be dismissed as sour grapes. All I can say is that I was no more interested in them—with their pre-yuppie good looks (exactly as I imagine Dan Quayle in college)—than they were in me.

I became more political with the era, and so did my boyfriends. There was a time when the Democratic Party was too conservative for us; like most pseudo-radicals, however, we came back to it when there didn't seem anywhere else to go.

The question "Were you for Robert Kennedy or Eugene McCarthy?" has come up on a surprising number of first dates in recent years. I find myself more attracted to the Kennedy men, though I was for McCarthy.

From what I can tell, people in their twenties don't talk about politics on the first date or any other date. I get the sense they don't think it matters. If they were making a list of what they were looking for in another person, his or her party affiliation probably wouldn't even get mentioned. It would be on my list, though, right up at the top with integrity and a laugh I like to listen to. Political philosophy reveals as much about a person as family background—possibly more, since you have a choice in the former.

This may be a minority opinion in a time when "Undecided" has become the third major party and people describe themselves as vaguely Democratic or vaguely Republican. But to me a man's politics do matter. Because of my background and the impact the 1960s had on me, I can't imagine being with anyone who looks at the world the way George Bush does. I am not ruling out the possibility that someday I will meet a Republican who will win my heart. But he will never win my mind.

Weddings Complete the Family Circle

I was supposed to be the flower girl at my cousin Allen's wedding, but I came down with chicken pox. It upset me terribly to be left behind. Even at seven years old, I didn't want to miss out on anything.

I cried myself to sleep, and when I awoke, the bride and groom were standing over me. They had come straight from the reception so I could at least see them. They looked as if they had stepped out of one of those fairy tales I loved to have read to me. I was too young to understand much about weddings, but I remember deciding they must be magic to turn my cousin into Prince Charming.

I thought about that as Allen's daughter, Rhonda, marched down the aisle. She looked as ethereal in white silk and lace as her mother had thirty-six years before. It has taken me that many years to understand the real magic of weddings. They are the pivotal event that brings families full circle. There I was watching Rhonda get married alongside relatives who could remember the day my parents got married and the day I was born, just as I could remember the day Rhonda's parents had married and the day she was born.

The problem with attending such a singular event as a single person (beside having nobody to dance with) is that you feel you aren't doing your part to assure the cycle will continue. I felt that way without any prodding from relatives. I suspect they may have given up on me. Not one of them asked, "So, when are you going to get married?" as they used to whenever they had the chance. They didn't so much as ask if I had a boyfriend. Nor did they suggest I join the group of young women eagerly waiting to catch the bouquet—which was just as well, since I had no interest in wrestling a thirty-year-old for it.

But I did suddenly have an interest in marriage. Weddings always have that effect on me. Other people cry at them; I want to settle down. I found myself nodding when the rabbi said, "According to the Scriptures, we are not meant to live alone. We were meant to share. We are stronger if we begin the task of living with someone else."

At that moment, I agreed with him—the same woman who has argued endlessly that *alone* is just as good as *together*, and that you'd better not wait for someone else to begin to live.

I can't look at a bride without redesigning her gown so it would look good on me. The dress in my mind is white and has a train, and I don't care what Emily Post says is appropriate for divorcées. I think about which music I would select for the ceremony. (It certainly wouldn't be the pop songs everyone seems to be choosing. I would leave the altar the proper way, to the Mendelssohn march—not to "What Are You Doing the Rest of Your Life?")

It has occurred to me that my longing may be more for a big wedding with all the trimmings than an actual marriage. That could be because I have had the latter but not the former. In the 1960s, when I was married, elaborate ceremonies weren't exactly in vogue. My Aunt Thelma, the family member most concerned with tradition, tried to convince me to have one anyway, but I wouldn't listen. So not only have I let the family down by not fulfilling my role as wife and mother, I haven't even given them a wedding to remember me by.

My position on weddings has come full circle. They seem as magical to me now as they did when I was seven. The rituals I used to find so hokey, such as cutting the cake once for the crowd and again for the photographer, now appeal to me precisely because I have watched generations of brides and grooms go through them. I love singing the same ethnic songs and dancing the same dances at every wedding. I don't even mind hearing the same family stories.

As you get older, you realize that the only occasions that bring the entire family together are weddings and funerals, and since you're going to have to be there at the sad times, you may as well be there at the happy ones.

Of course, while all weddings, like fairy tales, end happily, all marriages do not. My family has had its share of divorces, mine among them. But that's not what I was thinking during Rhonda's wedding. I was thinking mushy thoughts. Weddings have a way of doing that to you.

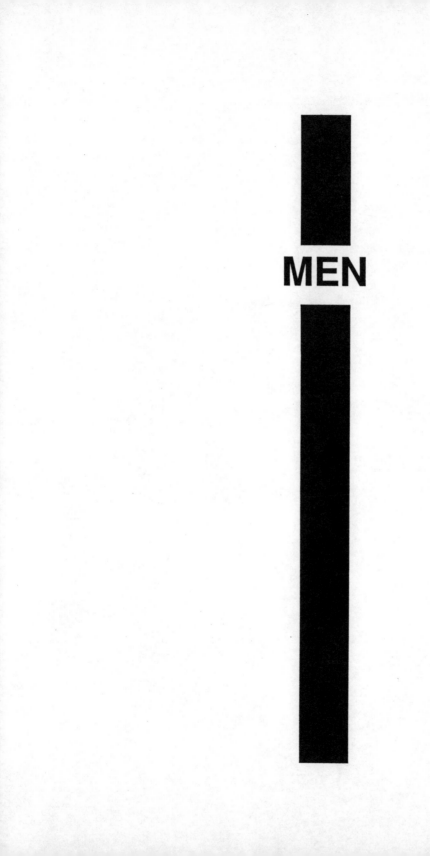

MEN

Sometimes it seems as if the sexes don't speak the same language. The "I'll call you tomorrow" line, for example, clearly means something different to the men who deliver it, lying through their teeth, than it does to the women who want so much to believe it. If men can't be taken at their word, why should they be believed when they say they never intend to get married? The right woman just might be able to convince a confirmed bachelor to change his mind.

It takes all kinds of men. Some are duplicitous, but just as many are kind and straightforward. The trick is to be able to tell one from the other. There are tip-offs single women should be aware of. One is to never trust a man who says, "Trust me."

We've Got Your Number, Don Juan

"I'll call you," says Dom, after a long good-night kiss at your doorstep. "I'll call you," says Dirk, at the end of a lovely day exploring the wine country together. "I'll call you," says Barry, tiptoeing out of your bedroom in the middle of the night.

So how come you never hear from Dom, Dirk and Barry again? Mind you, the question I am asking is not why don't they call. That's easy. They don't want to. The question is: Why do they say "I'll call you" when they don't mean it?

No single statement has led to as much misunderstanding and rancor between the sexes as this one. Since the invention of the phone machine, you can't even fantasize that he called you when you were in the shower.

One possibility is that men and women are simply speaking a different language. To him, "I'll call you" may be a polite way of saying, "Drop dead," while you want to believe those three words mean "I can hardly wait until the next time I see you." So, if this is driving you crazy, whom should you complain to: a shrink or a semanticist?

To learn about the origin of the Big White Lie, I went to the liars themselves. They hang around singles bars, waiting to tell some gullible woman, "I'll call you." The men seemed eager to talk and weren't at all defensive. They didn't think they had done anything wrong. When I asked them, they all understood the question immediately, even the ugly ones. It's like men are born with an extra gene for the Big Lie.

Here it is, right from the source, the reasons men don't call when they say they will:

• *Garry, thirty, salesman for a medical supply company:* "Women have this way of making you feel obligated to say something. I mean I meet a gal and I'm really not interested in her, I just want to have fun for an evening. I feel she is putting pressure on me to say something. So I say 'I'll call you' just to be nice."

You're quite a guy, Garry.

• *Peter, twenty-four, real estate agent:* "The circumstances usually are that I was drunk and there were sexual feelings involved that failed to resurface the next day. At the time, there was a feeling of goodwill towards that individual. But the next day, there was just a void."

And she didn't think you were so hot, either.

• *Steve, forty-one, bond broker:* "I say it when I think I'll never see the woman again. It's like a little white lie, so you don't hurt their feelings and to get you off the hook. No, I don't lie to my clients. I'm going to see them again."

• *Jim, twenty-six, salesman for Xerox:* "Yeah, I've told women that I'd call them. I was sincere at the time I said it. It just never materialized. Probably I met someone else and forgot all about the other woman. I've never thought that she might be waiting around for me to call. It would be pretty silly for anyone to sit by the phone waiting."

If the phone doesn't ring, you'll know it's Jim.

• *John, thirty-one, computer salesman:* "Sometimes, I'll strike up a conversation with a woman. The next thing I know, she's offered me her phone number, unasked. Just to be polite, I take it. Then I say, 'I'll call you.' It's just an easy way out."

• *Bill, forty-two, photographer:* "It seemed like the thing to do at the time, the way the conversation was going. I think some women take it too seriously. They take it a lot differently and more seriously than men mean it."

• *Larry, thirty-one, salesman:* "I might have just blurted it out. I would feel bad about it for a while, but not terrible. It's not like you broke someone's heart or something. We're all entitled to change our minds."

And I thought that was only a woman's prerogative!

• *Ken, thirty-four, IBM salesman:* "Sometimes when I say 'I'll give you a call,' I mean it. But as I have a chance to reflect, I realize that although I had a good time, there is no point to calling her because we really don't have much in common. I don't look at 'I'll call you' as a commitment or anything."

• *Alex, thirty, unemployed:* "The further I get away from her and the longer I wait to call, the harder it is. If I just met this person for the first time, I become shy about calling her."

• *Craig, twenty-nine, sales manager for a tennis company:* "If I have fun with a woman, even if I never intend to call her, I tell her that I will. I feel as if it's an obligation."

• *Mike, forty-five, lawyer:* "It's a minor lie compared to the way women lie. I think lying is built into their nature. They say they're interested in you sexually, but you'd better not try anything. They say they want to see you again: that is, until somebody better comes along. Saying you're going to call is damn slight punishment for everything women do."

Or, as Rhett said to Scarlett, "Frankly, my dear, I don't give a damn."

• *Steve, thirty-four, unemployed:* "If I don't intend to see someone again, I say, 'See you next time' instead of 'I'll call you.' That way I'm covered, because next time could be any time."

There they are, a dozen rationalizations for the one lie. Clip them out. The next time a man says, "I'll call you," you can tell him all the reasons he won't.

Why Men Still Can't Be Trusted

By now, women have wised up to the "I'll call you tomorrow" line and other statements men make that they don't really mean. But it isn't only their words that take a code to decipher; it's also the weird things they do.

I got a semi-hysterical phone call from a girlfriend. She had run into this man, in whom she has more than a passing interest, at a party and . . .

But let her tell it:

"He came over as soon as he saw me. We were talking—small talk about work and what we had been up to since the last time we saw each other—when suddenly he moved closer and put his hand on my hip as if we had just spent the night together.

"I should have excused myself and walked away. But I liked the way his hand felt. I was sure he was signaling me he was interested, and I wanted him to know I was, too. We stood that way for maybe ten minutes. Before we parted, he whispered he would call soon.

"I haven't heard a word from him. I feel like I've been defrauded. His gesture was so intimate. How could he not have meant anything by it?"

I know just how she feels. There are certain men whose intentions still puzzle me though I haven't seen them in years.

There's Evan, an intense young man (by young, I mean younger than I am) I sat next to at a chamber music concert. Like me, he had come alone. We discovered we had remarkably similar tastes in music. We had even been at some of the same performances before—each of us alone. "It must be kismet," he said. As dumb a line as that was, I fell for it.

The next weekend, he called and asked me to meet him for dinner in his neighborhood. He sounded as if he couldn't wait to see me. I put on my best first-date outfit, doused myself with perfume and took a cab over in case he wanted to take me home.

When I got there, Evan was already seated in a booth with an intimidatingly attractive woman. From his introduction, it was clear they hadn't bumped into each other at the restaurant. She had been invited to dinner. What wasn't clear was *why*. Was she his girlfriend and, if so, whatever gave him the idea I would want to meet her? I already know enough women. Or was she a friend called in to evaluate me—in which case I must have failed the test, because I never heard from Evan again.

Then there's Robert, who was taking a fiction writing class at the school where I teach. We got to talking at the coffee machine, and he asked if I would read his short stories and tell him what

I thought. I explained that fiction wasn't my field, but he was so insistent that I finally agreed. When I told my friend Mark about this, he laughed. "The stories are a ruse," he said. "Robert doesn't want your literary opinion. He wants to go out with you."

Of course, Mark was right. Men intuitively understand other men's intentions. But I still don't get why Robert didn't ask me out to begin with (thereby saving me from his earnest but plodding prose). Was he trying to flatter me by soliciting my advice? Or did he expect to win me over like Cyrano de Bergerac with the beauty of his words?

Mark tells me I should have more compassion for men. It isn't easy to always be the one doing the asking. He says men are terribly vulnerable, though they try to hide it. The things they do that seem odd to me are actually their attempts to protect themselves.

Perhaps. But there's got to be a better way than one that leaves women hurt, or at the very least confused. I wish it were possible to sit down with a man and ask him what he really meant. However, I know I couldn't bring myself to initiate such a conversation. I doubt many women could. I can't imagine my girlfriend ever asking, "So what were you feeling at the exact moment you put your hand on my hip?"

Women need a Rosetta stone to tell them how to read a touch—or whether to read a story.

They say "No Way" to "I Do"

His voice had that "I'm not alone" tone, so I told Tom to call me back and hung up fast.

When we finally spoke, he said it was "highly ironic" that when I'd phoned to ask if women take him at his word that he has no intention of marrying, he was in the middle of a heavy-duty discussion with his current girlfriend on that very subject. Their relationship was on the verge of breaking up—as all his others had—over the marriage issue.

Tom, a forty-one-year-old computer programmer, was married for a year in his twenties—long enough to know it wasn't for him. He says he makes that perfectly clear to women. Inevitably, they say they understand. Some of them even say they, too, prefer being single. But in no time at all they are pleading with him to change his mind and marry them.

Having heard the same story from countless single men, I'm convinced it has the makings of a bestseller. I already have a title: *Men Who Don't Want to Marry, and the Women Who Don't Believe Them.*

Tom moved here from Washington, D.C., ten years ago to get away from one such woman. They were living together when she began to mention the possibility of marriage. Even after he split, she kept calling him in San Francisco to talk marriage. "It was a six-month guilt trip over the phone," he recalled.

The beginning of the end for another girlfriend came the night she stopped by Tom's house unexpectedly.

"I guess I wasn't as responsive as she was hoping for, and she got angry," he told me. "That started a general argument that led her to admit that in fact she had not been completely honest with me or with herself—that she did want marriage and kids. I said I hadn't changed my feelings on the matter. We just called it off."

Joshua, a thirty-three-year-old musician, tells women he is a confirmed bachelor right at the start, so that there's no misunderstanding. "Sometimes I say it on the first date, like: 'Seen any good movies lately? What was your last lover like? I'm not interested in getting married.' "

Apparently some women see it as a challenge when a man professes not to be the marrying kind. It's as if he'd admitted to being an alcoholic. Women think if only they'll stick it out, they'll reform him. Men in turn are amazed at how they can tell a woman "No" a hundred times and slam the phone down in her ear—and still she won't give up.

"Women are unrelenting," said Martin, at thirty-two another ineligible bachelor content with a nomad life as a photographer.

"It's like they know what is good for you better than you do." He has had women use every ploy to win him over, including repeated offers of dinner. His response to their invitations "depends on whether or not I'm hungry."

Mike, forty-five, a San Francisco lawyer who has taken to heart George Bernard Shaw's advice that a man not married by forty shouldn't consider doing so after, admits to having mixed emotions when women try to get him to the altar. "Part of me is panicked about being entrapped and part of me is flattered. It's nice to have a woman think you are that desirable. But it gets to be a pain in the a— when they don't let up." He says he has done everything to discourage them, from writing long, thoughtful letters explaining his point of view to not responding at all.

None of these men held out the slightest hope of changing their minds—not even when I told them about this guy I know who, three days after telling Laura he would be single forever, was buying an engagement ring for Charlotte.

The men who don't want to marry talk a great game. But you know something? I'm not sure I believe them.

Troubles Can Multiply When a Two-Timer Tells All

Each time a romantic song was played at the pops concert, the woman next to me would take the hand of the man across the picnic table from her and get that dopey in-love look on her face. As one who is always trying to figure out relationships, I couldn't help noticing that the object of her affection didn't seem nearly as smitten.

At intermission, she got up, but he just sat there smiling at me and my date, Mark. The next thing we knew, he was filling our glasses with some very good wine he had brought along and telling us how he was in San Francisco for six weeks to get special treatments for a skin condition.

His friend, he said, pointing in the direction of the empty

chair, had come here from Phoenix to keep him company. Before her, another friend had visited him. He leaned closer to us and winked. The woman who was with him tonight, he said, doesn't know about the other woman.

I tried digesting that along with what was left of my turkey sandwich. Neither went down very well. I felt as if Mark and I had been made privy to information we had no business knowing. And for what possible reason? The only one I could think of was that our tablemate couldn't resist the chance to brag about his two lady friends—even if it meant making one of them appear foolish to people she didn't even know.

When she returned, I realized how young she was, surely no more than twenty-five and at least ten years younger than the man she was with. I felt she needed to be protected from him. I wanted to take her aside and tell her to dump this cad or at least let her know that he was two-timing her. Instead, I did nothing. I sat quietly through the rest of the program, telling myself it was her affair, not mine, though that didn't stop me from cringing every time she made eyes at him.

When it was over, I warmly said good-bye to her and ignored him. I doubt he noticed, since my friend Mark, a habitually nice guy, was patting him on the back and wishing him a good visit and good health.

I couldn't wait to unload my feelings on Mark. Didn't he think that man had been a complete jerk? How could he have been so indiscreet? Didn't Mark feel sorry for the poor woman? Mark seemed surprised by my reaction. Yes, he said, he had thought it a little odd that we had been told so much so soon. But the way he figured it, the young woman in question was probably in San Francisco only because the man in question had paid for her airline ticket. For all we knew, she had another boyfriend back in Phoenix.

I didn't buy that for a moment. I know the look of love—and she had it. She would have gotten here if she'd had to walk. But even if Mark were right, I couldn't imagine a scenario in which the roles of the two people at our table would be reversed. It was inconceivable that had he been the one to leave at the break, she then would have turned to us and told us about the other man she was seeing, whom this man knew nothing about. Women don't do things like this.

Nobody should. It is incredibly tacky and insensitive. Not only is it unfair to your date, but also to the innocent people drawn into your little soap opera. Besides, you never can tell about the people you might blab to. One of them could turn out to be a singles columnist.

Love Him or Leave Him? Some Subtle Tip-Offs

There are so many advice books for the lovelorn with double-decker titles that I can't keep them all straight. They've merged into one book I call *Women Who Love the Men Who Hate Women Too Much: Working Out Relationships That Will Never Work Out.*

Another entry in the advice sweepstakes is *Women Men Love, Women Men Leave,* brought to you by the duo, Dr. Connell Cowan and Dr. Melvyn Kinder, who wrote *Smart Women, Foolish Choices.* I wonder how they divided up the work. Do you suppose Cowan did *Smart Women* and *Women Men Love,* leaving Kinder with *Foolish Choices* and *Women Men Leave*? Their recent guidebook, like most others of its ilk, puts women into categories, which I suppose is one way to put them in their place.

The authors tell us men love a seductress (she lets a man know she is interested in sex), confidante (she's a good sounding-board for his ideas) and free spirit (she has a contagious passion for life). On the other hand, men leave an eager beaver (she starts talking marriage on the first date), ice queen (she turns off in bed) and spoilsport (she won't let a guy have any fun).

So, what about men? You don't have to play the dating game too long to realize that they fall into types as well. Here's how I'd categorize the men women love:

• The Sensitive Guy: He really listens when you talk. He writes you poetry—usually bad—but that only makes it more endearing. He never talks about other women in your company. (*Tip-off that he's that kind of guy: He calls the day after the first time.*)

• The Ken Doll: He doesn't give a hoot about clothes, but lets you dress him because he knows it matters to you. He pretends to be interested when you take him shopping. (*Tip-off: When you buy him a sweater, he immediately puts it on and wears it for days.*)

• The Professor: He knows all sorts of things you don't and is delighted to share his knowledge, though never in a patronizing way. He gives you books on your birthday that you actually want to read. (*Tip-off: You stay up all night on your first date talking.*)

And here are the men women leave:

• The Controller: He plans all the dates and yawns when you suggest an activity. He tells you how to drive. He even tells you how to cross the street. (*Tip-off: The first time he comes to call, he rearranges something in your house.*)

• The Non-Socializer: He wants to leave a party almost as soon as he gets there. He makes no attempt to talk to your friends. He says he would rather be alone with you, but doesn't have much to say even then. (*Tip-off: He doesn't seem to have any friends of his own.*)

• The Egomaniac: He talks about himself all the time. You get a blow-by-blow description of his day at the office, including every little injustice done to him. However, he never asks about your day. After months of dating, it's not clear he even knows what you do. (*Tip-off: When you pass by a mirror, notice where his eyes go.*)

And finally a special category, for the kind of man women love, but should leave:

• The Cad: He never calls when he says he's going to. He expects you to drop everything if he wants to see you. He tells you he has been away on business, and you find out he took a trip with another woman. (*Tip-off: The first time you make dinner for him, he shows up an hour late and doesn't bother to apologize.*)

Single Men Who Aren't Afraid of Sex Are Not Extinct

Since two young men moved in downstairs, I have felt like James Stewart in *Rear Window*. No, I don't spend my evenings peering into their apartment through binoculars. But because my rear window is next to an air shaft, I can't help hearing everything that goes on down there. What I hear are female voices. I hear women talking to my neighbors over dinner, and over breakfast. I hear women leaving sexy messages on their answering machine. Rarely do I hear the same voice twice.

And I thought dating had slowed down—that fear of AIDS had forced singles to be monogamous, if not celibate. Hadn't my neighbors been informed that promiscuity was out, or could all those women be their cousins?

The only way to find out what was going on in Apartment One was to ask the occupants. They seemed willing, even eager, to talk. We arranged to get together on a Saturday morning when they were not otherwise engaged. I brought muffins and a pot of coffee to their place; it looked as if they were waiting for their mothers to come and pick up after them.

Both my downstairs neighbors are named Bob, both are twenty-six and both are very cute, with boyish grins that women must find irresistible.

Bob One is a stock trader. Bob Two is just back from a trip around the world and is working in construction until he saves enough money to take off again. Wearing, respectively, a Lacoste polo shirt and a Hard Rock Café T-shirt, the two Bobs looked like a yuppie billboard.

Bob One got right to the point. He said the AIDS scare hasn't had much effect on his sex life: "I could go to a bar and go home with a girl as easy as I did four years ago." He didn't sound as if he were bragging, just being honest.

The big difference now is condoms—not just that he keeps them on hand, but that he is open about it. It used to be that if a woman found out he was carrying a condom, she would accuse him of being a sleaze—and having only one thing on his mind. These days, he gets points for being sensitive and caring about her.

When the Bobs were setting up housekeeping, they bought a canister set and filled the flour container—because it was the biggest one—with condoms. They never use flour anyway.

Singles bars are still the easiest places to meet women, they said, though the night before they had had great luck at a nightclub, dancing with one woman after another.

On the coffee table in the Bobs' living room was a paper napkin on which one of those women had scrawled her phone number and presented it to Bob Two. He had written "Hawaiian-Japanese" next to the number, so he would remember who she was. Bob Two said that he'd told her he would call and, being a man of his word, he intended to.

The same night, Bob One had come to the rescue of a pretty blonde whom at least a dozen guys were putting the make on. He told her their aggressiveness made him feel embarrassed to be a man. He swore to me he hadn't meant it as a line, but it seemed to have had that effect. She asked him to walk her to her car and then handed him a deposit slip with her phone number on it. Bob One couldn't help noticing a man's name was also on it. She admitted she was married, but said she was having marital problems and would really like to see him again.

Bob One told me that while he had a rule about not going out with married women, he probably would call her, just because he had the feeling she needed to talk. He wanted to make it clear that he and his buddy don't sleep with just anyone. "We could have had a couple of girls sitting here right now," he said, as I tried to imagine all of us sitting around talking about sex in the '90s. "But we didn't do it. We're getting a little old for that."

They also don't put any pressure on women to sleep with

them right away. In fact, they kind of like it when a woman holds out. It makes it so much more special, they said. Eventually the Bobs hope to meet women they want to settle down with. If someone like that were to come along, it would change their lives dramatically. "We couldn't be kissing other women and playing around," Bob Two said. "We have to just decide that's what we want and get out of the bar scene."

When that happens, I should be the first to know. It will get awfully quiet outside my rear window.

He Really Did Take a Chance on Love

When David told me he was marrying a French woman he barely knew and moving to Paris, part of me—the romantic part that wants to believe in love at first sight—thought, "Terrific, go for it!" But the part that clings to security reacted much as did David's mother, who, informed of his precipitous decision, screeched: "You're giving up a good job—with benefits."

David actually gave up more than a promising career as a TV producer in San Francisco. His life was busy bordering on frantic—which was the way he seemed to like it. He was known around town as "Mr. First Nighter." He would show up at openings and parties in the company of one lovely woman after another. If David was ever lonely or longed to settle down, he didn't mention it, though he used to talk about how much he loved "chasing skirts." (This would be said with such an endearing smile that it was impossible for his women friends, including me, to take offense.)

Then he met Catherine, who had only to say his name in her sexy French accent for him to fall in love, and they rode off—I suppose "flew off" would be more accurate—into the sunset.

I often wondered what happened. From Christmas cards, I knew David already had two children, that he was struggling with French and didn't have a steady job—certainly nothing with benefits. But those are just facts. I wanted to know about feelings. Was David happy? Did he feel he had done the right thing? Does love at first sight last?

When I was in Paris, I visited him at his house. (Actually, it's Catherine's house; the reason *he* made the move instead of *her* is that she had a better-paying job and owned her own home.) I was immediately struck by how David, who had always looked like a kid, now looked like a grown-up. I made polite conversation with his wife and oohed and aahed over their son and daughter. But David and I didn't really talk until the next day, when the two of us got together at a café.

The stars were definitely out of his eyes. He admitted that what he felt the first time he saw Catherine was more lust than love, but she was so certain they should "go for all the marbles" that she finally won him over. She also insisted they have children right away. She told David that if they didn't, the marriage wouldn't last, that he would get fed up with hassling with the French language and the French people and leave. She promised their children would be beautiful—which they certainly are.

David said he had always wanted a family but wouldn't have had one so quickly if it hadn't been for Catherine. "I was just thirty-three when we met. I had a few more good years to be single."

He can't believe how his life has changed. He went from living alone to living with four people, including an *au pair*. "I have no privacy. There's always someone around demanding attention."

Mr. First Nighter almost never goes out. It's expensive, and besides, when he isn't working, he feels he should be with his kids. He worries that he is turning into his parents. "I come home every night and turn on the TV." Still, David says he is happy most of the time and has no regrets. He and Catherine have a solid relationship based, he said, on complete trust, and he gets an enormous kick out of being a father.

I left the café thinking about the vagaries of life. A chance encounter and David was on the other side of the Atlantic with a family. Then I thought again: His changed circumstances are not so much the result of an encounter as the fact that he acted on it.

I know people who have had a similar encounter but weren't willing to go for it, and other people who were, except that their lover panicked and ran away. Here's the big question: Is what David and Catherine have the real thing, or is it just that they agreed it was and are now intent on making it work?

I am not advocating going for it. As I've said, I have a cautious streak. But if you don't take the risks, you'll never know whether there are any benefits.

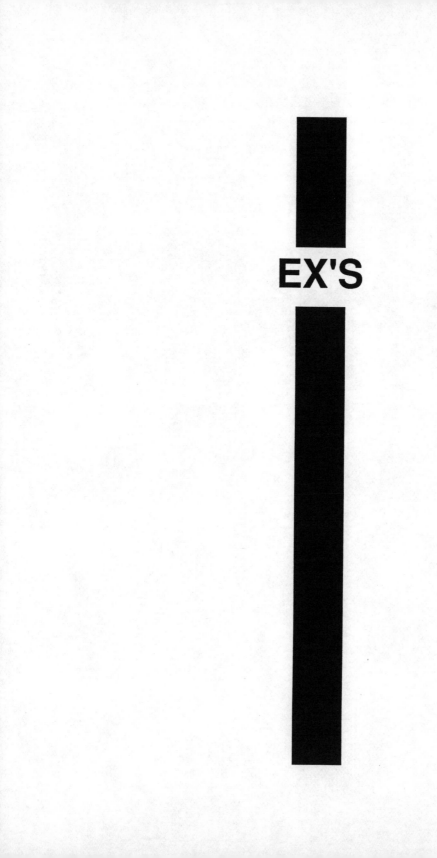

EX'S

They have acquired the unfortunate label "baggage." But they are not objects. They are the people we once loved and may even have married. In these times when serial affairs are in vogue, we will be acquiring a lot of ex's along the way. Memories of them cannot be tossed away as easily as the little gifts they left behind or the photos of the two of you in happier days.

You have to figure out what kind of a relationship, if any, you want to have not only with your ex, but with his or her family. Even if you never want to see this other person again, there's always the possibility you will run into each other. How you handle the reunion says a lot about both of you.

In time, you may wonder what you ever saw in him or her. Did you change, or did your ex?

Wondering Where the Love Went

He had left his first and last name, which I suppose was appropriate, considering how long it had been since we'd talked. Still, when I got back to my office and saw the message from him, I had to laugh. This was the man I was once willing to move to Philadelphia to be near; *that alone* qualified me as a woman who loved too much. Now it appeared we were no longer on a first-name basis.

The phone number on the pink message slip was local. So, he was in town and probably expected to see me. I had to think about whether I wanted to see him.

It's funny how a romance isn't really over when it's over. My friend from Philadelphia and I broke up in 1981. But for years afterward I would get a twinge at any mention of him. The last time he had contacted me—it must have been three years ago—I felt nervous and irritated at the realization that he could still get to me. This time I had no particular feeling. I returned his call, I guess out of respect for what we had once meant to each other, and agreed to dinner, probably for the same reason.

I did not, however, rush home and change into something wonderful. I went straight from work, stopping in the powder room only long enough to give my makeup and hair a perfunctory once-over. That wasn't residual love; I would have done the same had I been going to the movies.

I'd told him to meet me at a neighborhood hangout. I wanted to be surrounded by noise and people I knew, so there would be no suggestion of an intimate rendezvous. He was late. "How like him," I thought, remembering other nights when I had been kept waiting—nights when it had mattered a lot more than it did now.

When he finally arrived, I was startled by how out of shape

he looked. We used to joke about his soft underbelly, but it was no longer a laughing matter. He ordered a glass of champagne, which struck me as wrong for the occasion, and immediately began telling me everything he had been up to. He had always been a talker, but his stories, which I had once found endlessly charming, now seemed merely endless. Some of them also sounded familiar, as if I had heard them eight years ago.

I felt as though I were interrupting his monologue whenever I tried to interject anything about myself. He listened in that distracted way people do when they are just waiting for the chance to turn the conversation back to themselves.

I stared hard into his face trying to see what I had once seen in him. Whatever it had been, it wasn't there anymore. I was like Titania in *A Midsummer Night's Dream* after the love potion had worn off. How could I have felt so much for this long-winded, rather boring fellow seated across the table? Had he been a different person back then, or had I? And where, I wondered, had all those feelings gone?

He insisted on walking me home. To be polite and because not to have done so would have made it seem that I had something to fear, I invited him up. I knew he was looking around to see if I had kept any of the things he had given me. I pointed out a jewelry box of his. I could afford to be generous. He didn't stay very long—the only indication I had that he was at all sensitive to my mood. At the door, he gave me a bear hug. I stiffened visibly. He said, "'bye," and walked out of my life, I sensed, forever.

I sat on the couch for the longest time trying to make myself feel. Like a sleepwalker, I went over to the stereo and put on the song that I used to play in the last days of our romance. Suddenly the room was flooded with reassuring voice of Nat King Cole: "There will be many other nights like this," Nat crooned. "And I'll be standing here with someone new. There will be other songs to sing, another fall, another spring. But there will never be another you."

At last, I felt something. I felt sad.

The Past—in Presents and Pictures

One of the first things I did as a newly *un*married woman was to throw away all the photographs of my former husband and me in happier times. Watching twelve years of memories float down the garbage chute, I must have thought: "Well, that's that; now I can start over." Of course, if it were really that easy to dispose of your past, shrinks would be out of business. Yet whenever you come to the end of an affair, the temptation is to get rid of everything that reminds you of it, as if that will somehow wipe the slate clean.

The homes of single people are like temporary exhibition galleries. For an indeterminate period, you display the Teddy bear or heart-shaped paperweight your new love gave you for Valentine's Day and put pictures of the two of you up on every wall. Then he or she stops calling, and the show comes down. Your scissors are poised, ready to cut the jerk out of the photos. Teddy and the other mementos are stuffed into a paper sack on their way to the incinerator or to be dumped at the doorstep of the person who dumped you. (The latter is what those how-to-end-a-relationship books are always advising you to do.)

I would urge you to stop short of actual destruction. Haul the memorabilia down to the basement if you can't stand the sight of it. But hang on to it. The time will come when you'll want to look at it again without having to guess the identity of the cutout figure.

To recast a piece of advice about life: This is your past—not a dress rehearsal. At some point, you have to claim it or risk that terrible sense of disconnectedness that seems especially to afflict singles.

When my friend Suzy gets nostalgic leafing through some-body else's wedding album, she goes home and takes down both of her albums from a back shelf where they were long ago relegated. That strikes her as a much better way to remember her husbands than at the time of the divorces.

However, as a result of my precipitous action, I have no visual record of my married life. It's as if it never happened. There ought somehow to be some reminder that it did.

I learned my lesson and have since become a great hoarder of the stuff of romances. The tricky part is figuring out what to do with it. I know one woman who has hung photos of herself with former boyfriends in her entry hall. She calls it her rogues' gallery. I've always wanted to know, but have been too polite to ask, what her gentlemen callers make of it.

I think it's probably wiser to keep the pictures to yourself. Mine are filed away in manila folders. (O.K., so I'm a little compulsive.) A guy has to stick around to rate his own folder; the others are filed under "Misc." I also have large yellow envelopes filled with notes and cards and little things that once meant a lot.

The presents I put out, since I'm the only one who knows how I came by them. My Teddy, from a dear, sweet man about whom I have only nice memories, has a place of honor on top of the bookcase, alongside several other stuffed animals whose purchasers are not so fondly remembered. On a shelf below is a picture of me taken by a photographer with whom I was quite smitten at the time. I am smiling broadly, showing too many teeth. I like looking at that photo, though it's not especially flattering.

In my kitchen there's an oval terra-cotta casserole dish. Each time I use it, I recall the snowy Chicago day when a man gave it to me as a way of saying he was sorry. I won't say what he was sorry about; but I will allow that it was an appropriate response.

Years ago, I went shopping with a friend for a chair for her boyfriend, who had moved into a new apartment. We must have looked at a hundred chairs before she settled on one. I happened to be at that man's home recently. He is married to someone else, but he still has the chair.

Gifts like that once said, "I love you." By keeping them around, you can hear the echo.

When You Run Into an Old Flame

Once we went to theater openings together. Now we go separately, each of us pretending the other isn't there. My seat is in a direct line behind his, so I can study him unobserved. I see that his hair is getting thinner, and his women younger. Sometimes at intermission, I sense him near me, and I become more animated. I tell snappy stories rather loudly. It is a performance as he—the intended audience—must surely realize.

Ideally, you would break up with someone and that would be it—the last of him or her. But unless you plan to move to another state, it is inevitable that you will run into each other again. So it becomes a matter of how you behave during these encounters.

I have a theory about that. I think it's out of your control. Whether you want to or not, you will behave much the same way you did in the relationship. For instance, I acted like an adolescent when I was going out with the balding man at the theater. I met him right after my divorce, a ripe time for a second adolescence. I'm embarrassed to think of the stupid things I said and did.

I want to tell him, "Listen, I'm not like that anymore. I've grown up." But how do you say that in a theater lobby? Instead, I make a point of not talking to him and of trying to get him to notice me, neither of which exactly qualifies as grown-up behavior.

(The man under discussion doesn't talk to me, either, but I wouldn't presume to explain his behavior. If he were a gentleman, he would spare me the discomfort by staying away from theaters on opening night.)

Should you bump into an old flame, it is a natural response to want to appear to be prospering. You're communicating the message *I can do very well without you*. However, when two people have had a competitive relationship, they are more likely to want to spell out just how much better off they are now.

I know a woman who split from her boyfriend because she couldn't stand it that he beat her at most sports and made a lot more money. When she heard they were going to be at the same party, she bought a very expensive dress and invited the best-looking man she could scrounge up to be her escort. She also arranged to have several people at the party mention to her ex that she had gotten a promotion. As it turned out, he never showed up, the ultimate one-upmanship.

Accidental meetings can be a disaster for competitive types. Their idea of hell would be to go to a movie alone on a Saturday night in running clothes and wind up in line behind an ex and his or her date.

If a relationship isn't really over—which is to say one person is still stuck on the other—seeing him or her can be disastrous. A meeting rekindles all those feelings you are trying to forget. You are apt to behave badly, make a scene and all that. My advice would be not to say anything and to leave quietly.

At the other extreme are the terribly civilized encounters in which both parties trip over their words in an effort to be polite. I was with a male friend when he ran into a woman he had almost married. He introduced her to me, and we stood around and made sophisticated small talk like characters out of a Noel Coward play. There was no indication that two of the characters had once been in love. That was typical of their relationship, which had also been terribly civilized. It died of too much civility. It might have lasted if they had occasionally thrown things, or at least raised their voices.

The best chance encounters are, predictably, between people who had the best relationships. They seem genuinely glad to see each other. They talk easily and openly of the past and present. They are delighted, not envious, if the other person is doing well. They want to continue the conversation as long as they can, instead of trying to get out of it. The big question about reunions like that is why the couple ever broke up.

Breaking Up Isn't So Very Hard to Do

I'm for anything that injects a little humor into what is too often a melancholy time for singles: the end of a love affair. So I'm tickled that Hallmark has come out with a line of greeting cards for the occasion. Look for one that reads, "Breaking off a relationship is like eating Thanksgiving leftovers. . . . You're better off when the turkey's gone!" It could be your special way of saying good riddance to the turkey of your choice.

We need to lighten up about breaking up, if we're to survive being single over the long haul. Consider that "serial relationships" (an odd coupling of words—when I hear serial, I think "killer") are going to be big in the '90s. Since you can't marry everyone you're relating to, even serially, that means most of these relationships are destined for oblivion.

If you treat every breakup as if it were a death in the family, you'll spend much of the decade unhappy—a state of mind to which I am philosophically opposed. My desire to be happy has allowed me to bounce back even when *I've* been the one dumped.

I wonder whether watching your parents split up, as I did, makes you more resilient: You learn early that people you love don't always stick around, and that you'll be O.K. without them. You also learn to get on with life.

The day after my college sweetheart and I broke up, I joined a computer dating service called Operation Match. (Trivia aside: It was run by Douglas Ginsburg, the allegedly dope-smoking U.S. Supreme Court Justice nominee.) I was matched up with my ex. Deciding it was fate, we married, only to get divorced. That taught me never to trust a computer in matters of the heart.

In case Hallmark is interested, I have another axiom about breaking up: Don't take longer getting over a romance than the romance itself took.

I learned this lesson from my friend Karen. She has an

unfortunate habit of falling for jerks who keep her on a string for a few months and then leave in some hideously cruel way. As each one departs, Karen becomes convinced that he was the love of her life. She is inconsolable for months. I know this as one who has tried to console her. She thinks she will never meet anyone else like him. If only that were true.

Some advice:

• *If you feel as if it's time to walk, it probably is.* Somewhere—probably from married couples—singles have gotten the notion that every relationship is worth trying to save. However, to me a big advantage of being single is that you don't have children or other encumbrances to make you stay together. The only reason to do so is because you want to. When you no longer want to, you should feel free to split. A sure sign is when other people start looking good.

• *Reject his (or her) rejection.* Let's say your lover has broken up with you. Tell yourself you're wonderful, and he or she has made a terrible mistake. Be specific about the ways in which you're wonderful—your high intelligence, zany sense of humor, well-formed biceps, for example. If you can't think of any, it's no wonder you were rejected.

• *Do anything you feel like (as long as it's legal) to help you get over the relationship.* This includes having a fling. I know the party line is not to get involved with anyone right away. I say let your emotions be your guide. If you're attracted to someone, go for it. I've done this myself. Though the romance didn't last, it helped me get my mind off the person I wanted to forget.

• *Don't listen to any songs about the heartbreak of breaking up.* Dionne Warwick seems to specialize in this genre. The last thing you need is to hear her sing "Make it easy on yourself . . . 'cause breaking up is so very hard to do." It doesn't have to be. Honest.

The Sleaziest Way to Leave Your Lover

Two more men have been reported missing, and those are just the ones I heard about.

While I listened to these tearful accounts of boyfriends inexplicably disappearing, like ships or planes in the Bermuda Triangle, thousands of other jilted women were no doubt recounting their tales of woe to anyone who would sympathize with them.

The first woman I had to console was my manicurist in Hawaii, where I had gone to get away from the angst of single life. I handed my fingernails to Maggie, and her sad story came spilling out with the polish remover. She met Tim on the beach. (I gather that's where he spent most of his time.) She convinced him to move into her place, and for six months all was bliss between them, at least according to Maggie. One day while she was at work, filing away, Tim packed up his belongings and cleared out. Just like that. Gone with the ocean breeze.

When I got back from Hawaii, my friend Sally rushed over to report, between sobs, the disappearance of her boyfriend, Brad. Brad is no beach bum. He's an accountant, a responsible person who isn't supposed to do flaky things such as vanish. They'd been going out for a year. The subject of marriage had been broached, always by Sally, though she swears Brad didn't blanch.

On their last date, he dropped her off early, saying he had a headache. She called to see how he was doing. He wasn't home. She left a message on his machine. He didn't respond. A few days later, a messenger delivered a box to her office. In it were the robe and slippers she kept at Brad's apartment.

I couldn't tell which upset Sally and Maggie more: their men's leaving or the way they left with no explanation.

Married men have also been known to disappear. I have another friend whose husband went out for beer during halftime and didn't come back. She had one small consolation: She got the house. Joe Montana's ex-wife blabbed to the *National Enquirer* that Joe kissed her good-bye one morning and waved as he drove away, never to return.

Women may not always know how to end a relationship gracefully, but I don't believe they're capable of pulling a disappearing act. They have almost a biological need to talk it over, to analyze what went wrong or confess that they've met someone else. It could be that women talk *too* much. Some things really are better left unsaid. But at least they let a man know why he has been dumped.

The common complaint about men is that they're afraid to confront their feelings. This could explain the missing boyfriend phenomenon, though I think there's more to it. Men are better at cutting their losses. They've been trained to walk away from an impending deal when they realize it isn't going to close. To explain all the reasons why would take too much of their valuable time.

I've been able to find a few missing men. It wasn't hard. They rarely go far. They weren't the slightest bit ashamed. They didn't think they had done anything wrong. One of the missing—a novelist who presumably has a way with words—asked me, "What is there to say? The question is why women would want to discuss it? When it's over, it's over."

What should Maggie and Sally and all the other discarded women do? They could track down their errant men and confront them. This kind of confrontation almost always has an ulterior motive. The woman wants her Houdini back, despite what he did to her. She shouldn't hold her breath. A man driven to disappear is not going to come back just because he's asked. Instead, the two of you will have a conversation you'll both regret later. If he couldn't think of anything to say before he left, the right words are not going to come to him weeks later. He'll probably clam up—that is if he doesn't hang up.

My advice would be to let a missing man stay missing. You're really not missing much.

Breakups Mean Losing a Family, Too

Shortly after my husband and I separated in 1978, I phoned his mother to wish her a Happy New Year. I guess I was testing the waters. I wanted to see if this woman, who had always insisted on my calling her "Mom" still thought of me as kin. Her icy tone was chilling evidence that as far as she was concerned we weren't even acquaintances anymore.

That was my last contact with the in-laws until I received a letter from Shari, my former niece (if there is such a thing). She had discovered my singles column in a paper in Colorado and "could really relate to it," she wrote. It was a shock to realize that Shari is old enough to be dating, since in my mind she was still ten, the age she had been the last time I saw her.

I called her immediately and, without intending to, wound up grilling her about my long-lost relatives. I hadn't realized how hungry I was for news of them, or how shut out of their lives I felt.

Talking to Shari has made me nostalgic for the families of other men I've been close to. I wonder what's become of Kevin's mother, who showed up in hot pink the first time we met—after I had ruled out wearing red because it might seem too brassy. I also wonder about Gary's brother, the one who seemed as if he would never find himself, and about Robert's daughter, who was just starting to trust me when her dad and I broke up.

When relationships end, the relations depart along with the spouse or significant other. Their loyalty is to their kin as, of course, it should be. I wouldn't want my sister to continue to be chummy with any of my ex's.

Still, that's an awful lot of people to suddenly disappear from your life. It's disconcerting to realize just how tenuous these connections are and that you can go from being practically a member of the family to *persona non grata* overnight. You are likely to be put through this wrenching experience any number of times, now that relationships take so many forms—live-in, long-term, committed, noncommitted—that have a greater potential than marriage for winding up kaput.

One way to avoid the rejection would be to avoid the relatives altogether. However, I can't imagine myself doing that. Like others who grew up in a broken home, I've always sought out surrogate families, not run from them. I'm adept at ingratiating myself with people's folks and getting from them what I didn't get from my own family. I was the kid parents wanted their children to play with, and I became the woman they all want their sons to marry.

I've rarely had to spend a holiday alone; there's usually been a boyfriend eager to take me home with him. I've felt so much a part of the family that I halfway expect to be invited back after the romance ends. However, as I get older, I find I'm no longer being introduced to a beau's parents but to his children, and they are not so easy to impress. They have no particular reason to like me and have plenty of reasons not to. They've already been through one divorce and seen what it has done to them and to their father. They are not going to get too close to me and leave themselves vulnerable to being hurt again.

I can't really blame them. This generation's children of divorce understand the transitory nature of relationships better than mine did.

I suppose we could all learn from them to be better at protecting ourselves. But what would be the point? If you care about someone, the natural instinct is to want to bond with his family. The alternative seems pretty gloomy.

Once, at a dinner party, I was seated next to a very wise woman in her eighties. She had done things the old-fashioned way: one husband, one set of in-laws, no affairs. After hearing a tale of modern romance, she leaned over and said, "People lead such untidy lives these days."

Indeed we do. A path strewn with ex-surrogate families is one of the prices to be paid.

Don't Call That Ex

Sometimes I get an urge to call an old boyfriend. Maybe I have just had some good news and, out of habit, he's the first person I want to tell it to. Or maybe I've run across a photo of us from the last trip we took together or a book he left at my house, and suddenly I'm desperate to hear his voice.

I try to stay away from phones until the urge passes. It's too risky to call out of the blue. What if he didn't recognize my voice? It would be awful to have to identify myself after all we've been through. Worse yet, suppose he had met another woman with my name and had to ask, "Ruthe who?" We would undoubtedly end up having one of those awkward conversations that people have who used to trust each other but no longer do. There are the pregnant pauses and the listening between the lines, as one person tries to figure out what the other really wants.

A simple "How are you?" could sound like prying, to a suspicious ex. Is the purpose of the question to learn if he is going out with anyone? Or are you honestly interested in how he is? No matter what you might tell yourself, these calls are rarely innocent. There is almost always an ulterior motive. You should think about what you really want before you start to dial.

The longer you are single, the more ex's you are likely to acquire. They just lurk there in your past. The easiest thing to do about them is nothing. It's not like high school, when you would break up and then have to sit next to each other in algebra class. Unless you work together—and you'll find out fast why office romances are a mistake if yours ends badly—you can and probably should just drift apart.

However, I know how hard it is to let go completely. I haven't loved that many men to be willing to have one of them completely disappear from my life. It seems strange that someone who was so central to your existence could suddenly become a non-person, like a Soviet leader who has fallen out of favor. Your friends—the same ones who used to listen to you talk about him endlessly—are careful not to mention his name. You get rid of everything he ever gave you.

You can try to stay friends, though in my experience that's been hard to pull off. I don't want to hear about the wonderful new woman my ex-boyfriend is going out with. I'm not that mature.

The buddy-buddy approach strikes me as a throwback to the '70s, when everybody was supposed to be one big happy family. During that period, my friend Lois got the idea to invite both her ex-boyfriend and her current one to dinner. She thought they might like to meet each other. Why she thought that, I'm not exactly sure. I was also invited, and I can tell you it was one of the most uncomfortable meals I have ever sat through. The two men had nothing to say to each other.

On the other hand, I have another friend who for years has spent Christmas with the man she used to live with and his wife. They all get along famously.

When most people break up, they reach some sort of compromise between having no contact at all and being chums. They exchange birthday cards, make the occasional phone call, get together for the occasional drink. Eventually, even this stops.

The feelings, though, never stop. I know a woman who had no contact for twenty years with a man she almost married except for a subscription to *The New Yorker* he sent her every year on her birthday. One year, the magazine stopped. That was how she found out he had died. She locked herself in her bedroom and cried. She had always thought they would talk again.

Ex-Husband's Baby Ends the Hopes

Anne and I have been friends so long that even long-distance I could tell from her voice that something was bothering her. When we had gotten past the chitchat, she told me what it was. She just heard her ex-husband's new wife was pregnant.

Anybody who has been married knows what devastating

news that can be. No matter how many years it has been since you last saw your ex or how you feel about him or her, a pregnancy ends your marriage with a finality that divorce papers and remarriage can't quite equal. For Anne, the situation was complicated by the fact that she had never stopped loving her former husband. I knew them both in college and used to envy how much in love they seemed. I think their marriage would have lasted if they hadn't rushed into it when they were barely twenty and had lived so little.

Anne had been a virgin when they married (that might sound quaint now, but in the mid-'60s, nice girls waited), and the sexual revolution, which already was gestating without our knowing it, would be too great a temptation for her.

I listened to Anne complain that she didn't want to go through life having slept with only one man; then I listened to accounts of the affairs she was having. By the middle '70s, her marriage was in a shambles and so was she. Anne survived, even prospered, on her own. But she had always thought that somehow she and her husband would get back together after she'd had enough of being single.

She called me when Elizabeth Taylor and Richard Burton remarried, as if to say, "See, these things do happen." She did not phone when they divorced again.

While Anne never actually went after her ex—she has been too busy with other relationships—she didn't let go of him either, even after he married again three years ago. They talk on the phone every few months and see each other whenever one is in the other's city. Anne tells me his wife has never said a word about their friendship, though I am not as convinced as Anne that it has not been a problem for her.

But now that wife No. Two is with child, everything has changed. Anne's fantasy, which most likely never would have been realized anyway, has been wrenched from her. While she might have imagined herself breaking up a marriage, she couldn't possibly consider breaking up a family.

I have not fantasized about getting together again with my

former husband; yet I was still upset when his wife had a baby. I heard it from my housekeeper, who had worked for us when we were married and thus, unlike me, had received a birth announcement. (Did my ex not send me one to spare my feelings? A more Machiavellian interpretation is that he sent her the announcement knowing she would tell me.)

My feelings were exacerbated by how competitive I have always been with my husband. That didn't end with the divorce. Not only had he beaten me to the altar, he had also won the baby race. (Never mind that those things no longer interest me; what I am talking about is not rational.) It was as if when we divided things up, I got the ashtray and he got the family.

At the same time, I also felt happy for him. He was, after all, someone whose happiness once mattered quite a bit to me, and I was pleased to realize that that hadn't ended with the divorce.

Anne was now experiencing the same ambivalence. Her husband, who came from a large Irish-Catholic family, had always wanted children. In the early years of their marriage, he had lobbied for them to start reproducing soon—a thought that terrified her since she didn't feel anywhere near ready (and still doesn't). She told me a part of her was delighted for him, just as another part could hardly stand it. (It's even worse for a divorced woman who wanted a child during her marriage only to be put off by her husband, who then has a baby with his second wife.)

Anne used the word "closure" in describing how she felt about the news. "That's it," she said. "That's closure on our marriage." She seemed to say it with regret. I would say (though I didn't, being a tactful person) it's about time.

How Not to End Years of Not Being Married

Sondra Locke couldn't have made Clint Eastwood's day by socking him with a palimony suit, and she didn't make mine, either. I was sorry to see their relationship end in a flurry of court documents and tabloid headlines. I had hoped it was about more than money and houses (though when one person is very rich and the other isn't, inevitably it seems to come down to that). This is one Hollywood romance that actually interests me. I've been tracking it since the beginning and have my own reasons for desiring a less sleazy finale.

In 1976, I went on a press junket to Santa Fe for the premiere of *The Outlaw Josey Wales*, the first movie Locke made with Eastwood. Considering the rumors that were circulating about the two of them—and the fact that he was married at the time and, it turns out, she was, too—Locke was remarkably cool talking to reporters. I remember thinking that if there were any truth to the rumors, the inscrutable actor had met his match.

Because very little was written about them in the thirteen years they were together (Eastwood would never say anything about his personal life, which is ironic in light of the dirt that came out), I could project my own fantasy onto their relationship. I imagined they had something going that gave them the support of a marriage with none of the constraints—in other words, that they had figured out how to be married and single at the same time.

As one who has experimented with that kind of relationship and knows how ticklish it can be, I welcomed all the famous role models I could find.

It was hard to keep looking to those longtime companions, Jean-Paul Sartre and Simone de Beauvoir, with both of them dead. Anyway, I never could quite envision them as intimates; it seemed as if they would get into some philosophical discussion and forget what they were doing.

I admired Eastwood and Locke for apparently not feeling the need to marry, but also for not falling into the trap many unwed couples do of living as though they were married. They maintained separate homes—his in Carmel, hers in L.A.—and separate lives. She was off directing a movie when he was sworn in as Mayor of Carmel.

Thanks to all the gossipy stories about Locke's lawsuit, my

illusion about them has been shattered, along with Eastwood's privacy. What I had thought was a model relationship has degenerated into another tawdry palimony case, where the woman is trying to soak her rich paramour for everything she can get. If it were a movie, it would be called *For a Few Million More*.

Instead of Ms. Independence, Locke describes herself as making her career subservient to Eastwood's and as living in a house that he owns, though she insists he gave it to her. She says he persuaded her to have two abortions and finally to have her tubes tied.

For all she claims to have given up, she is asking for unspecified damages, title to a couple of houses and half of everything the actor earned during their years together. I wonder if Locke realizes how foolish she sounds, at least to this independent woman.

If she thought she could have had such a hot career without Eastwood, why didn't she go for it? And, if the house in Los Angeles was really a gift, why didn't Locke get it put in her name? In my opinion, a woman who lives in a house owned by a man who sometimes stays with her and sleeps with her is being kept. I also have to question how Eastwood could possibly have talked her into giving up her ability to have children. What about her free will? Or did he revert to Dirty Harry and persuade her that way?

The whole mess points out how difficult it is to end a relationship that is like a marriage but not a marriage. Locke obviously wants something to show for the time she put into it. However, there are no clear-cut rules on what that something should be. I had hoped these two would be able to work it out between themselves. But Locke has chosen to play the helpless little lady and has brought in her attorneys in supporting roles. Not even Clint Eastwood could head them off at the pass.

LOOKIN' GOOD

Tt's our little secret, the amount of time you have to indulge yourself when you're single. If your fantasy is a day at the spa or something more exotic—say, a class on how to strip for your lover—go for it.

With no spouse or kids to attend to, you really have no excuse not to take care of yourself. Health clubs have become the '90s way to meet people, but before you get too carried away with all those (other) hard bodies, whip yours into shape by actually using the exercise equipment.

Developing a sense of style comes easier when you're the only one you have to please. By all means, keep up with the latest fashion. When you've really arrived, you'll be able to set your own. The real secret to looking good has nothing to do with the latest cream to smooth away wrinkles or plastic surgery to give you those luscious lips that are all the rage. The secret is to feel good about yourself. If you feel it, you'll just naturally look it.

The Evolution of a Personal Style

Like a mythological siren, Bloomingdale's beckoned me. "Come inside," it called, "and see what's here for you."

I had not gone to New York to shop. I had in mind loftier pursuits: the theater, modern art, a decent corned beef sandwich. However, I allowed myself to be lured into Bloomingdale's. I wanted to get a good look at and maybe even finger the "very sexy suede separates, sleek velvet dressy dresses and fuzzy fun parkas" that the fashion magazines (don't you just love the way they put things?) extolled for fall.

What I really wanted was to see whether any of these clothes were me, or at least the person I am this season—which is not necessarily the person I was last fall and certainly not the person I was a dozen falls ago.

Back then, I was a married person, specifically a doctor's wife, who dressed accordingly in white blouses with Peter Pan collars and midi-length muted paisley skirts. Toward the end of my marriage, I bought a red sundress that revealed a lot of back as well as leg. It was more a red flag than a frock. (I never forget an item of clothing. I am like the socialite about whom it was said: "When she dies, her wardrobe will flash in front of her.")

Clothes have continued to signal who I am. They chart my progression as a single woman, from the insecure early years when I dressed to please men—Victorian lace one Saturday night, black leather the next—to a sustained period of pleasing only myself. During the latter, I've developed what I think of as a singular sense of style, combining fashion know-how with a refusal to take the whole thing terribly seriously.

For instance, when drab dress-for-success suits were fashionable, I would wear mine with iridescent spike heels, as if to say, "Only kidding about the suit." And when miniskirts came back, I was the first in my crowd to put one on. I dismissed the notion I might be too old; I felt younger than I had the first time minis were in style. I still don't understand what it means to dress your age.

Wandering through Bloomingdale's, I felt equally at home in the junior department as in the one for grown-ups. Money was no object, because I didn't intend to buy anything. I rarely ever do until January, when the prices are slashed, and I can afford to look like a rich lady if that's how I happen to feel. I was, in the words salespeople are loathe to hear, "just looking." But I was looking with special antenna, able to distinguish what was me from what wasn't.

Here's how I divide the latest fashions:

• Transparent chiffon blouses: Not me. I can show a little thigh, but I have my limits. On the other hand, I admire women who have the courage as well as the equipment to pull it off.
• Red suits suitable for the office: Me. Red is the new power color, and I'm all for it. Here's where women executives have it over men. Can you imagine one of them showing up in a red business suit?
• Suede jackets with fringe: Not me. I predict these won't go over big with the generation that came of age in the '60s. They look too much like what Dennis Hopper wore in *Easy Rider*.
• Gold studs on everything from parkas to cocktail dresses: Me. I like the idea of adding glitz to ordinary attire.
• Long skirts in muted paisleys: Not me. This look has regrettably returned under the rubric "the new traditionalist." Reminds me too much of my married days.
• Plain white T-shirt and jeans: Me. Especially since seeing how great the combination looks on models and movie stars.
• The fling—a shawl or large scarf tossed over the shoulder: Not

me. (Also, not what comes to mind when I hear the word "fling.")
I've never been able to figure out how to wear one of these and
not look as if I'm being choked.
• Animal prints: Definitely me. I'm especially wild about leopard spots, which I think are terribly sexy. Men think so, too. Trust
me. In fact, a leopard-print dress is my one purchase so far this
season. I've had a leopard sweater and belt for years. You might
say leopard has been me for a long time.

Things You Must Not Do
for Love

I once dated a man who liked to see me in ruffled blouses and
peasant skirts. I didn't own anything vaguely like that when
we met, but I was crazy enough about him to fill my closet with
frilly things.

Those clothes have long since been disposed of, as has the
man. It is obvious to me now that our romance never had a
chance. I could put on ruffles to please him. But I could not
ultimately become the sort of woman who would dress that
way—which was what he really wanted.

Having been there, I understand the temptation to transform
yourself for another person. It seems a small price to pay to get
him or her to stick around. However, in my lucid moments when
I am not going around humming "What I Did for Love," I think
even the smallest change is probably a mistake. Once you start
chipping away at who you are, you risk losing someone far more
important than a suitor. That someone is you.

There is a basic contradiction here. We all dream of being
loved just the way we are. Yet when we fall in love, we want to
play Pygmalion and mold that person to conform to an image we
have of perfection. I have heard of actual physical alterations
done in the name of love. The brunettes who became blondes are
nothing compared to those who have had their noses done or
their chins lifted or fat surgically removed from wherever on

their bodies it had been deemed offensive.

The futility of all this became apparent to me when I heard about a woman who got silicone injection at her boyfriend's request—only to have him leave her for someone with even larger breasts.

It's just as stupid, if less obvious, to alter your basic beliefs because your honey asks you to. Where does such wishy-washy behavior stop? If you could go from being a Democrat to a Republican—as Ronald Reagan is said to have done for Nancy—does that mean you would switch back or become a Socialist if somebody more appealing came along?

I know too many women who converted to Judaism in order to be accepted by their Jewish boyfriends and particularly the men's families. They would dutifully march off to the rabbi's study several times a week to learn how to be a Jewish wife. Excuse me for being skeptical about these shotgun conversions. If your own religion matters so little that you would give it up so easily, then I have to question what meaning another religion could possibly hold for you.

I'm not saying one should never make accommodations because of love, but, rather, that love should not be contingent on these.

My friend Margo learned this the hard way when she tried to convince the man with whom she was living to marry her. He wanted a woman who would cook and take care of him like his mother had done for his father. Margo is terrific in all kinds of ways, but frankly, she has never been much of a homemaker. She tried so hard to please him that it was almost painful to watch.

I remember the six-course dinner she prepared mainly to prove her culinary talents to him. She even made bagels. Nobody makes bagels. Predictably, the meal was a disaster. Instead of teasing Margo about it, as everybody else at the table did, her boyfriend sat there scowling at her. I don't think he said a word to her all evening. Not long after, he moved out.

There is an important lesson here for all of us. You can't make yourself over into someone you're not, and nobody should expect you to try—especially not a person who is supposed to love you. Bob Dylan put it better. There comes a time when you have to look that someone in the eye and say, "It ain't me, babe, it ain't me you're looking for. . . ."

Clothes Make the First Date

There are people who will tell you they never think about what to wear on a date. Do not believe them. They are the same people who used to brag about how they never studied for an exam. *Everybody* thinks about it. By everybody I mean men, too. The only question is how much time it takes them to decide and how many outfits they try on in the process.

I equate the level of anxiety over how I look with the depth of my feelings. I know I'm really crazy about someone if I experience a moment of panic right before he arrives, in which none of my clothes will do and I want to rush out and buy something new. My other test is the number of trips to the mirror to check my makeup. The most I ever counted was twelve. The man in question was very late, and I was very nervous.

The point is, you're *supposed* to be a little obsessed with your appearance, especially on a first date. If you don't care enough then to make an effort to look terrific, I predict there won't be a second. Assuming the two of you hardly know each other, the way you dress is going to make a greater impression than perhaps it should. There isn't much else to go on at this point. You should give some thought to what your clothes will say about you.

It's always risky to attempt to look sexy, because your idea of sexy may not be the same as your date's. For example, if a man were to show up at my door with his shirt unbuttoned to his waist and a gold chain around his neck, I would think twice about letting him in.

I am far from a conservative dresser, but I do dress that way in the beginning and save the miniskirts and black leather for later. I have a feeling that the latest fashions intimidate a lot of men. I know I would feel uncomfortable going out with someone who looked like a model for *Gentlemen's Quarterly*—not that that's ever happened or has been likely to. It's safer to affect a casual look, as if you just stepped out of the shower and grabbed the first thing in your closet—although this is not as easy as it sounds and could take hours to get right.

My friend Steve has the "first-date look" down. He puts on a coat and tie because he believes he looks better in them. However, so that he doesn't appear to have made any special effort, the tie is always old and worn; the jacket, casual. The shirt is blue, to match his eyes. He thinks women respond to that color on him. So much for men not giving any thought to what they wear!

If you can learn to dress for success, you can certainly learn to dress for a date. Here are some do's and don'ts to start you out.

• Do find an outfit you feel great in and stick with it. Turn it into your first-date uniform. However, if you find yourself in it every Saturday night, you must be doing something wrong.
• Don't wear something new the first time you go out with someone. It might not fit, and you'll be pulling or tugging at it all evening. You have enough to worry about without that. Besides, to a new person all your clothes will be new.
• Do confer with your date beforehand on where you are going and the appropriate dress. There is no worse feeling than getting all gussied up only to have him or her show up in jeans and a sweatshirt.
• Don't make so many changes in your appearance that you no longer look like the person who was asked out. Women have been known to re-do their hair completely and put on so much makeup that their dates wonder if they are at the right house.
• Do allow enough time to get ready, so you are not frazzled. You never want to start out on a date breathless. The time for that is later.
• Don't spend the entire evening worrying about how you look. You've done the best you can, so relax and enjoy yourself.

Women Strip Down to Their Fantasies

The teacher began by saying she did not intend to be long-winded. She believed we would learn, not from listening to a lot of highfalutin theories, but from practice. "So, I'm going to have you stripping in ten minutes," said Fanny Fatale (obviously not our instructor's real name).

In less time than that, we—the twenty-five women enrolled in "How to Strip for Your Lover," an adult education course with a triple X—were lined up in an exercise studio ready to take it off. Actually, we weren't supposed to take it *all* off. This was, so to speak, a dress rehearsal for the real striptease we were to do for our boyfriends.

We had been told to wear a leotard, over which we piled some combination of these strippable items: a garter belt, bra, feather boa, one nylon stocking, one long glove and dangling beads. Most of us had come to the 7 p.m. class straight from work, in tailored suits. Looking around at the getups, I thought, "If our employers could see us now."

Fanny, whose seven years experience as a professional stripper amply qualified her to stand before us, asked us why we were here. My classmates were as uninhibited about responding as they would prove to be about everything else: "I'm Alice, and I've always had a fantasy about being a stripper." "I'm Joanne, and I can't strip for my sweetie without cracking up. I thought if I learned the moves, I would be more professional about it." "I'm Sally, and I just look on it as a handy skill." "I'm Ruthe, and I hope to get a column out of it."

(What I was too shy to admit was that I, too, have had the stripping fantasy. I suspect many women have—which may be why the $29 course has been a sellout wherever it's been given.)

Fanny suggested selecting three songs and putting them on one tape, so we wouldn't have to interrupt our performance to change the music. She also suggested we wear layers of clothing. "Two sets of underwear, for instance, is a nice surprise. And you might want to put your hair up, because it's nice to take it down and whirl it around later."

However, she cautioned us, to do that right would require at least four songs. You never want to rush through a strip. "The trick is to be very slow and tease."

The moment had come when we were to try our hand—and, it turned out, our teeth—at it. Fanny demonstrated how to undo a button the sexy way by curving your fingers around it and popping it with your thumb. Suddenly, I was all thumbs. I checked out the rest of the class. We looked more like a bunch of toddlers struggling to undress ourselves than would-be strippers doing it for pleasure.

Gloves were much easier, probably because they were the last thing to go. By then, we had taken off blouse, bras, boas and beads and been repeatedly told by Fanny to "think sexy."

Following teacher's lead, I bit the top of my long black leather glove, a remnant from some long-forgotten party, and pulled it all the way down with my teeth. "Run it down your body, over your breast and your hip, then throw it off," she suggested. I did all that, and I "thought sexy." "Oh, gloves are just the funnest things," said Fanny, who talks in superlatives.

The final lesson was in what she called "floor work." I soon realized she didn't mean the same thing Jane Fonda does. As Fanny crawled and moved in ways best left undescribed, one student asked, "What are you wearing at this point?" "Nothing," Fanny said.

After class, the graduates of Stripping 101 discussed whether we would ever have the nerve to strip in front of a man. "Maybe if I had a lot to drink," said Sally. "Maybe if my boyfriend had had a lot to drink," said Alice. "Maybe it's better just to fantasize," said Ruthe.

Exercising One's Right to Exercise

I read a lot, and a lot of what I read turns out to be pretty stupid. Usually, I forget it the minute I'm done with it. However, something in a newspaper article so outraged me that I can't put it out of my mind. The story was about exercise addiction, a pretty bogus subject to begin with. In the course of making the strained argument that exercise can be as harmful as alcohol and drugs, the writer singled out one group of what she calls "exercise fanatics."

"Single professionals would rather hit the streets or the gym after work than confront an empty house," she concludes. "For some, workouts meet their needs for social contact; for others, exercising is a way to avoid thinking about an empty social calendar."

The assumption here is that there is something better for us single professionals to do with our time. We could stay home, for instance, and turn into couch potatoes like our married friends. Or we could load up our social calendars with heavy dinner dates (the meal, I mean, not the date) and late-night drinking and carousing. That's sure to do wonders for our health.

As one who works out every day and is proud of it, I have a different perspective on exercise and the single person. I think singles should take advantage of the fact that they have more time to keep their bodies in shape. I resent the implication that I do it to fill a void in my life. I feel perfectly comfortable coming home to an empty apartment, though I don't see much point in hanging out there. My social calendar is as full as I'd like it to be, thank you, and I have no interest in picking up a fellow jogger. That's the furthest thing from my mind when I'm running.

I exercise because I want to and because I believe it is not only good for me, but also quite possibly the best thing I do for myself. I consider myself lucky not to have the kind of major responsibilities that would preclude a regular exercise regimen. I know people who had to give up jogging or tennis when they had children and miss it as much as a good night's sleep.

I refuse to buy this writer's theory that there is a "darker side of exercise addiction," since it runs counter to everything I have been told and believe to be true. My internist says I have the cardiovascular system of a nineteen-year-old. My cholesterol level is just where it should be. The last time I got a massage, the woman asked me whether I was a dancer. Best of all, I feel great—all of which I attribute to exercise.

Yet, according to this anti-exercise propaganda, I am a serious addict. Without my daily fix of aerobics and a run, I would go into withdrawal and depression. I can see myself now, groping for my Nikes with a shaking hand or standing up at a Runners Anonymous meeting and confessing to being a four-mile-a-day run-a-holic.

I'm proud that I never miss a day of exercise. I call that discipline—not addiction. When I first started my regimen, nine years ago, I decided that if exercise weren't an ingrained habit, I'd find too many excuses to miss it. As it is, I break only for illness. If I have to be at work early, I get up that much earlier to have time to work out. I travel with my Jane Fonda tapes and have jogged in countries where people look at me so strangely they must think I am being chased.

This single-mindedness would be difficult for a spouse or even a traveling companion to take. On my own, however, I can do aerobics to my heart's content, and my heart seems very content, indeed.

If I'm an addict, then so are people who are into Transcendental Meditation and feel the need to recite a mantra several times a day. And what about those who run to the sink every morning to brush their teeth? That seems an obvious case of toothpaste addiction.

More obviously, a distinction needs to be made between habits that are good and those that are harmful. There just isn't room at the Betty Ford Center for every kind of addiction.

Besides, it would be hard for the staff to tell us exercise junkies from the other patients for whom exercise is desirable. Imagine the stampede if a counselor were to accidentally walk into one of our group sessions and suggest, "Tennis, anyone?"

Smoothing Out Worries of Wrinkles

Like a meticulous housekeeper who sees only the dirt she missed, when I look in a mirror I block out my good features and see just the wrinkles. There's one under my right eye—a deep line that lately seems to be sprouting antennae—and two more starting at the bottom of my nose and extending at an angle past my mouth. The latter type have been kindly referred to as laugh lines and, unkindly, as Howdy Doody lines.

Now it seems someone has come up with a magic potion that will make my wrinkles disappear like the picture of Dorian Gray. So what if the stuff is actually a skin cream used for the treatment of acne? Or that it is only supposed to do away with lines caused by the sun (and I have no idea if that was the culprit in my case)? I'm willing to take a chance, to believe in magic. To say to a tube of cream: "Go ahead, make me young."

I have been on the verge of badgering a dermatologist, any dermatologist, for a prescription for said cream. At the rate other people have been calling their doctors' offices, if I don't do so soon, there may not be any of it left. Yet I can't quite bring myself to make the call. One reason for my reluctance may be a recognition that the part of me that is obsessed with wrinkles is not the best part.

I should have other things on my mind, and I mostly do—as long as I stay away from mirrors. If I get the skin cream, I'll be peering into them constantly to see if it is doing any good.

Then, too, I am a purist about not fiddling with nature. I haven't touched the color of my hair since I doused it in peroxide as a teenager. It turned orange, and my mother made me leave it that way until the roots grew out. What's more, I have vowed that I will leave the gray in my hair, which I suppose is easy to say when you don't have any. I have also said—probably too many times, especially should I ever change my mind—that I will never have cosmetic surgery on any part of my body. Nobody is getting near my face with anything larger than a tweezer.

But there is another crucial reason why I am not lining up at the latest fountain of youth. I have to question for whom I am trying to look young.

I remember a rather sad woman I sat next to years ago on a flight. We had one of those intense conversations people have who know they will never see each other again. She was probably in her mid-forties—around the age I am now—and had obviously been a great beauty. She had been married, several times, as I recall. She told me she didn't mind not having a husband as long as men were attracted to her. But she was aware they no longer looked at her the way they once had. She worried about losing her looks and wondered what else she had to offer.

Certainly, there will be lots of single women like her clamoring for that miracle cream. They need the affirmation from men that comes with an unlined face. Not that married women don't also desire a more youthful appearance. But the need can't be as great, knowing that one man has promised to love you—wrinkles and all.

I suppose I had always taken it for granted that men would look at me to the point where I had stopped noticing. Now when I do catch a man's eye, I am startled by how old he appears, old enough in my mind to be my father. However, he is not looking at me in a way that could be construed as fatherly. I would like to think his eyesight is failing, and he has mistaken me for an older women. But I'm afraid I *am* an older woman.

Do I rub potions into my skin every day like a queen of ancient Egypt so men in their twenties will glance my way again? I have no interest in going out with guys that age. I have no idea what I would talk to them about . But neither do I want them to look past me as if I weren't there.

If I decide to try out that anti-wrinkle cream, it should be for my sake. But what would I really be gaining? I am not like that woman on the plane. I know I have other things to offer besides my looks. I wish they could invent a cream that would make my vanity disappear. I think *it* is the bigger problem.

Bewitching Secrets to Delay Aging

Myra is one of those people you wish you could hide from at parties. She used to seek me out across a crowded room to complain about being single. When she would fret about how there weren't any men, I was tempted to ask who she thought those creatures in neckties all around us were.

The last time Myra sidled up to me at a party, her complaining had developed a new wrinkle. She'd become obsessed with the notion she was aging badly.

She studied my face for signs of wear. Women often do this to each other, though rarely as blatantly as Myra's once-over. "It's not fair," she whined. "You're older than I am and you hardly have any wrinkles. What are your witching secrets?"

Before I could answer, Myra was telling me she had picked out a plastic surgeon and was saving her money to "go under the knife." She sounded as if she could hardly wait.

The range of options available to the Myras of the world, who can no longer face their faces, is impressive or alarming, depending on your point of view. It is now possible to have your forehead lifted with suction, your ears "re-created" (that's what the ad says) and the fatty tissue from your buttocks transferred to your mouth to give you those luscious lips that are all the rage.

If your perceived problem is below the neck, plastic surgeons will accommodate with tummy tightening, hip contouring and— this one really gets me—calf enlargement. (When *The Graduate* was tipped off that the future was in plastics, do you suppose this was what was meant?)

I think the problem for most people seeking this kind of surgery is in their head. I've thought that since I was a teenager and would visit a girlfriend who had just had her nose done. Her face would be black-and-blue and her eyes bloodshot. While telling her she looked great, I said to myself, "You'd have to be nuts to put yourself through this." Invariably, I liked my friends' noses better before the surgery. I feel the same way about face-lifts. They make people look unreal—plastic, if you will.

Mine seems to be a minority opinion. Cosmetic surgery has never been more popular. Even men are getting nipped and tucked. Articles report the emergence of "plastic-surgery junkies," who keep going back for further alterations. I wonder how many of these people are unhappy with their lives and taking it out on their faces. I know, for instance, that, deep down, Myra believes a wrinkle-free face is going to help her meet men. It won't. Only a personality transplant could accomplish that. In terms of being a panacea, a face-lift is bound to be a letdown.

I wish Myra had given me a chance to answer her question, because I do have some witching secrets. None involves plastic surgery. My face and I are going to grow old together.

My secrets are pretty basic, but they do appear to be working. For all the Myras and Myrons out there, these are for you:

• *Don't frown.* My mother told me this thirty years ago, and I'm convinced it's the reason I don't have a single wrinkle on my forehead. I do, however, have smile lines. I smile a lot.
• *Get some exercise every day*—preferably the kind that makes you sweat. I believe that's the best thing you can do for your skin.
• *Drink as much water as you can bear.* I'm up to a dozen glasses a day and have grown to actually like the stuff. Like it or not, it's great for your pores.
• *Sleep at least seven hours a night.* Here is where it helps not to have kids.
• *Keep learning.* If you don't do anything for your mind, it will show on your face. You won't get wrinkles, but you'll develop a vacant stare, which is much worse. I'm always reading good

books, taking classes and hanging out with people I can learn from.
• *Find something to be thankful for.* This witching secret comes from a friend (not Myra, needless to say) who is pushing fifty and looks fabulous. When her battery died as she was about to leave on a trip, she gave thanks that she had a car.
• *Stop worrying about aging.* Nothing ages you faster.

SO, WHAT ARE YOU DOING FOR THE HOLIDAYS?

I f you're ever going to get blue about being alone, it will probably be over the holidays. Festive occasions such as Christmas, Easter or Passover are sure to bring back memories of being with your parents and siblings and make you wish you had started a family of your own.

The way to fight the holiday blues is to surround yourself with friends. Throw a party—even if it's a birthday party for yourself. Just because you're single doesn't mean you can't establish holiday traditions. An especially nice tradition is to send out Christmas cards. So what if there's only one name on the bottom and no photo of a smiling family around a fireplace?

Valentine's Day causes a different kind of panic among

singles, who worry whether anyone will remember them. Again, you should take action. Send everyone you know a Valentine long before the big day, in the hope that a few people will get the hint.

A Card Just from Me

The first year I was married, I ordered elaborate Christmas cards, the kind with gold foil underlay, and had my husband's name engraved on them. I identified myself the old-fashioned way, as his "Mrs." The long, chatty notes on each card were written by me, but appeared to be penned by somebody called "We." There were mentions of how "We" had gone hiking in the Rockies and "We" had twenty people to Thanksgiving dinner and "We" were planning a trip to Mexico—all of it designed to create the impression that "We" were having a grand time.

The year my husband and I split up, I used my holiday cards to broadcast the news to anyone who hadn't already heard. I didn't actually write that "We" had gotten divorced. But only one name was on the bottom of the card, and there were no references to "We."

The next year, I didn't send cards at all. It was a difficult time for me, a time of coming to terms with being single. I didn't see how I could express those feelings on the bottom of a Christmas card, and I couldn't bring myself to pretend that everything was wonderful.

As a result of not hearing from me, friends from all over the country called to find out if I was all right. I was touched by their concern. It made me realize that I was not as alone as I felt. It also made me understand the significance of this once-a-year communication, especially with those people you like an awful lot, but hardly see anymore because they live so far away. A holiday card is a way—sometimes the only way—of staying in touch. No matter what syrupy message is inside, the real message is simply: I'm alive and well, or maybe not so well, but alive, nonetheless.

Yet I'm aware that single people often feel estranged from

this quite nice tradition. I mean, your friends start reproducing, and the next thing you know, you're getting photos on Christmas cards of happy families posed in front of fireplaces, accompanied by news of how Little Sally has started to talk. In my case, the news is that Little Sally has started college, which is a little unsettling, since in my mind her parents are still college age.

You wonder what you could possibly write that would be as significant as the achievements of their children. Somehow, a job promotion or European vacation pales in comparison.

Picking out my holiday cards, I realize how much I try to create an illusion of myself leading this terribly sophisticated life in San Francisco. It's as if I'm saying, O.K., I'm alone, but at least I'm stylishly alone. The cards I bought have a picture on the cover of a grand piano with a poinsettia on top. The color scheme is red and black. None of that mushy red and green for me.

One year, I sent out cards of the Manhattan skyline—for no apparent reason, since I did not then nor have I ever lived in Manhattan. Another card showed party-goers who looked like the crowd that hang out at the "21" club holding up glasses of champagne, with the greeting: "Here's to a good year!" I avoid family scenes, even if the family depicted is Mary, Joseph and Jesus. I leave the family stuff to my friends.

But I no longer feel like an egomaniac because the predominant pronoun on my notes to them is "I." I have become comfortable with "I." I am having, if not a grand time, a very good one. I think my friends will want to know that.

Inviting Lovers and Other Strangers

Like all great ideas, ours was startling in its simplicity. Here we were, two single women looking to meet men, with lots of friends also in the market and the holidays upon us.

"Let's put on a party," I said to Barbara, or maybe she said it to me. Perhaps we said it in unison, like Judy Garland and Mickey

Rooney. The idea wasn't original. A few Christmases ago, Barbara and Beth had given a "Party to Meet Men." Beth wound up marrying one of the guests—which is the equivalent of winding up with a royal flush at your own poker party.

With that precedent for inspiration, Barbara and I thought about whom to invite. We came up with four categories: the people she knew; the people I knew; the people we both knew; and the people neither of us knew. The latter group, we agreed, was critical. It was what fresh blood was to Dracula.

Asking strangers to a party is not as peculiar a notion as it might sound, though it does require imagination and courage. For instance, Barbara had long admired a local weatherman from the other side of her TV screen. They happened to have a mutual friend. Barbara sent this friend two invitations and asked her to pass one along to the weatherman. We waited to hear whether he was warm or cool to the idea.

I had fun mentally mixing and matching our guests. I'm not very good at one-on-one fix-ups. But the beauty of this kind of party was that you simply threw people together and let them pair off as they chose. However, neither Barbara nor I wanted it to be strictly a singles affair where everybody was so busy looking around that nobody had a good time. So we had invited married couples as well. We figured they'd set a good example.

Most of the RSVPs were from the couples. I don't know if they had better manners or if it was just harder for the singles to make plans—or if they were waiting for a better offer.

The party had put me in the holiday spirit early. I was already thinking about what I was going to wear. I'd raised the possibility of corsages with Barbara.

In the season of sharing, what could be nicer than sharing your friends? And what better way to make yourself feel good? I get so tired of the stories that come out this time of year about how miserable the holidays are for singles. These stories make us sound like a pretty pitiful lot just trying to survive until the New Year. I'm not denying this can be a tough time to be alone. But it can also be a tough time to be in an unhappy marriage or an

160

unhappy family. Despite what you may read, singles haven't cornered the market on feeling blue.

I'm enough of a Pollyanna to believe most people can cure themselves of the blues. One way is to put on a party; another is to go to all the ones to which you've been invited, and maybe even crash a few to which you haven't. Hardly anyone ever gets thrown out of a Christmas party.

If you know how to go about it, holiday parties can be terrific places to meet someone. Like anything else, there's an art to it.

• *Put yourself in a party mood.* What works for me is to wear something that makes me feel fabulous. You might have a different method. Anything is O.K., short of drugs.

• *Go alone.* It will force you to talk to people you don't know. If you come with a friend, you'll be tempted to spend the evening glued together, which practically ensures that you won't meet anyone.

• *Take risks.* Sashay up to someone you find attractive and say something. Almost anything will do. The point is to connect. If he or she doesn't want to play, you can always disappear into another room.

• *Stick it out.* If you're not connecting with anyone, the door is going to start looking pretty good. But you can never tell who might walk through it at any moment, so wait it out as long as you can.

Barbara and I put the word out to our single friends to come unaccompanied, but didn't allow them to leave that way. Our party was a big success. We have high hopes for the '90s.

Wrapping Up Love for Christmas

Jan had just entered the University of Chicago when we met. To me—a lowly high school junior—he seemed terribly grown-up and slightly dangerous, a combination I have continued to seek out in men.

Before our first Christmas together (it would also be our only one, although in the rush of romance, I must have thought we would go on like this forever), I spent days rummaging through stores for a present worthy of him. Finally I found it: a bulky russet-and-gold sweater as rugged-looking as he was. I gladly shelled out my life's savings for it.

For weeks, I waited for Jan to show up wearing The Sweater. He never did. When I got up the courage to ask about it, he reluctantly admitted that he had returned my gift. The tears had already formed in my eyes when he got around to adding that he hoped I didn't mind.

I learned a couple of chilling lessons that chilly Chicago evening: Anything you give to someone you really care about automatically becomes layered with meaning, and not all men are worth the attention you lavish on them.

Fortunately, this experience did not sour me on searching for the perfect present while still under the illusion that the recipient is the perfect man. The romantic in me believes you should care as desperately as O. Henry's heroine in "The Gift of the Magi," who cuts off her hair to buy her man a watch chain, not knowing he has sold his watch to get her combs for her hair. "I couldn't have lived through Christmas without giving you a present," she gushes to him.

How much energy you are willing to put into the search is a good gauge of how much this person means to you. If you buy the first item you see, especially at the beginning of a relationship, you should probably start shopping for a new beau.

It's a risky business to ultimately make a selection, and not just because your honey might not spend as much time or money getting you something—indeed, in the worst-case scenario, might not get you anything at all. You are saying to him or her: I believe I know you, and this gift is who I think you are. The present is your love in tangible form. It has to be personal. The only way to assure it will be is to choose it yourself, after pondering what you really know about this man.

It won't do to go shopping together or cop out with a gift certificate. The biggest cop-outs were those "For Men Only" boutiques in vogue a few seasons ago. A saleswoman picked out a present for a strange woman, while the man, who presumably knew her intimately, was being plied with liquor.

Some presents seem to be not so much for the person whose name is on the package as for someone you wish he or she would be. For instance, I was baffled by the clunky jewelry I received one Christmas from a man who shall remain nameless. He had never seen me in anything like it. Was he telling me he wanted me to wear jewelry like that? Much later, I found out about the other woman who received an identical gift from him that season, and was the clunky type.

I know women who see holiday gift-giving as a chance to dress their boyfriends, as if they were Ken dolls. Mr. Polyester winds up with a 100-percent wool suit under his tree. Men must resent this "I-know-better-than-you" attitude.

I have rarely given a man a book for Christmas, not because I find books impersonal, as some would hold, but because they are almost too personal. You are asking him to spend days or weeks reading something on your say-so. (Books are, after all, meant to be read, the popularity of coffee-table tomes notwithstanding.) Also, the books I would want to give haven't been in hardcover for 150 years, and a paperback lacks the weight to be a proper holiday gift.

If you're lucky at Christmas, you'll be spending the shopping days blissfully looking for a present that feels as right as the man for whom you're buying it. I can't advise you on what it should be. But I promise you'll know it when you see it. It will leap out at you—a gift of love, a gift of the Magi.

Alone with a Turkey

One Thanksgiving Day, when I was married, I went to the movies by myself. *Carrie* had just opened, and I was dying to see it. Somehow I couldn't convince my husband that a film about a shy teenage girl who uses her telekinetic powers to bump off the kids who have been mean to her was appropriate Thanksgiving Day fare.

I couldn't help noticing that almost all the people in the theater were alone. They sat several seats apart with their eyes glued to the screen before the movie had even started. There seemed to be an implicit understanding that if they didn't look at anyone, no one would look at them. Gradually, it dawned on me what those people were feeling. It was shame. They were ashamed of not having anywhere else to go on Thanksgiving.

Their attitude began getting to me. I wanted to shout at them that I wasn't like them. I had other plans: My husband and I were having Thanksgiving dinner at the home of our best friends. More friends were going to be there, along with children and dogs.

I didn't really say any of this. I simply left as soon as the film was over and ran back to my life.

That was the last time I went to a movie alone on Thanksgiving. Since my divorce, I have an almost morbid fear of being by myself on this holiday. It probably stems from an increased likelihood that I *could* wind up alone, now that no one is morally bound to spend the day with me, and my family is two thousand miles away.

In my worst-case fantasy, I imagine I have nowhere to go. I look into windows of happy homes, my nose pressed against the glass like the Little Match Girl. Eventually, I wind up at an out-of-the-way diner. I don't mean a trendy new one, but the seedy kind that Edward Hopper used to paint. I order the Blue-Plate Special for one: Thanksgiving dinner with all the trimmings, just $8.95. I am surrounded at separate tables by the people from the movie house, their eyes, this time, staring down at their gravy-soaked mashed potatoes.

So far, I have been spared such a fate. For several years, I spent Thanksgiving with the family of a guy I was going out with. It was wonderful to mingle with his relatives. I could observe the family dynamics without being involved in them, like watching *The Bill Cosby Show*. When that relationship ended, I halfway expected his family to continue including me. They didn't, but other people almost always have.

The one year that no invitation was forthcoming, I did the turkey myself and asked a bunch of my single friends over to share it. I'll do anything not to be alone—even cook. Yet no matter how many people are around me on the holiday, I can't stop thinking about those who are alone. I feel a "There-but-for-the-grace-of-God" connection to them.

Several times, I have thought of writing a newspaper story about their plight. I could hunt them down in darkened movie theaters and desolate diners. Hiding behind my reporter's notepad, I could ask them all those things that I am obsessed with knowing: What does it feel like to be alone on Thanksgiving? How did you end up this way? Don't you have any friends? What can I do to avoid your fate? But I have never followed through on the story idea. I would have to do it on Thanksgiving, and I have always had other plans.

Sometimes I think I should go ahead and live out my worst fantasy: Spend the day all by myself. Go to the movies alone. Go out to dinner alone. Go home alone. I might find that, like many of my fears, the reality isn't nearly as bad as I imagine it to be.

I should probably do just that. But not this Thanksgiving, thanks. I have other plans.

When You Care Enough to Say It in Writing

I know this is asking a lot and that singles should probably be grateful to get any Valentines at all. But wouldn't it be lovely to receive a card with a personal message instead of one composed by Hallmark? It wouldn't have to be anything elaborate. Your beau could describe your eyes or how he felt the last time you were together. What's important is that the words refer to your relationship alone instead of to generic relationships.

Hardly anyone takes the time to put intimate thoughts down

on paper anymore. It's too easy to phone them in or pick up a greeting card that supposedly says what's on your mind for you. I worry that note writing may already be an outmoded means of communicating. The best hope of appealing to the peripatetic high-tech generation could be an ad campaign pointing out that you can fax the same message to all your Valentines around the world.

If this has indeed become a lost art, generations to come will have no record of the great romances of our time—the way we were left the passionate correspondence between Elizabeth Barrett Browning and her hubby, Robert, for instance.

It's hard for me to imagine that Sonny and Cher exchanged heartfelt letters or that Cher has been courted via the mail by any of the lads she has taken up with since (several of whom may not be old enough to write). I also have my doubts that Tom Cruise remembered to pen a "Dear Mimi" letter to his wife before their much-publicized breakup.

There is something to be said for a written record of any romance, great or small. It's your chance for immortality. Think about your great-grandchildren rummaging through a trunk someday and coming upon the torrid words of one of your lovers, who was not their great-grandfather.

I'm quick to throw out receipts and canceled checks that I end up needing around tax time. However, I have held on to every scrap of writing ever sent to me by a man. You can't save everything, and I know what's important. I have a poem that Joel F. wrote on the spot, the evening we walked down to the beach. Some ten years later, I still remember the last line: "Waves crashed, and we stood together." As poetry, it was pretty prosaic; but as a romantic gesture, it was pure poetry.

I also have a letter from Joel dated a few months after we broke up. I had invited him to a party some girlfriends were giving, hoping he might meet someone. I accidentally put down the wrong date, and he showed up at their house a week late. It was clear from what he wrote that he thought I had done this on purpose, to embarrass him. He was hurt and confused and was willing to spill out his feelings on paper.

If he had called and screamed at me, I probably would have forgotten the incident long ago. But his written words serve as a reminder of the way in which love lingers and how gentle we have to be with it.

My friend Joan has a file folder stuffed with letters from a long-ago long-distance suitor. For a while, she got something in the mail from him every day. She would explain his fervor by saying, "He's married, and married men always try harder." As angry as she eventually became at him—adulterous affairs rarely end well—his letters still touch her. She knew what a risk he took writing them. He could have been blackmailed, like Bette Davis in *The Letter.*

There's a risk every time you write a love letter even if you don't have a spouse to hide it from. You are committing yourself on paper. Sure, there are quicker ways to communicate these days than with a pen. But I suspect that's not the only reason personal notes are becoming a thing of the past. A lot of singles are running from commitment. They've been battered by too many romances. They seem to be looking for Teflon relationships that can easily be slid in and out of. A love letter says you were there, and that you cared. And it goes on saying it forever.

Why Religious Holidays Are Not for Singles

Several Passovers ago, I invited all the single friends who would fit around my dining room table to a seder. I made the brisket, and they brought the chicken soup, matzo balls and potato kugel.

We did everything by the book—in this case, the Haggadah— yet our celebration fell flat, like unleavened bread. The Passover ritual calls for children, but there were none at our seder table. When it came time to ask the four questions—a role traditionally assumed by the youngest child—we all looked at each other quizzically.

The next seder I gave, I made sure to include a token child. Brian, a precocious seven-year-old, sailed through the four questions. He did not spill any red Mogen David wine on my off-white carpet. He left that to my friend Sylvia, who is five times his age. Though he would be too polite to say anything, Brian probably didn't have a great time. It couldn't have been very satisfying to hunt for the *afikoman* (a hidden piece of matzo) without any competition. I remember the thrill I got when I was seven and found it before my nine-year-old sister did.

I also remember learning from my mother, who taught Sunday School, why we ate matzo instead of leavened bread during Passover—to feel a bond with the ancient Hebrews, who had to leave Egypt so fast they couldn't wait for their bread to rise. But most of all, I remember the warm feeling of being with family.

I long for that again—the connection with my religious heritage, as well as the familial sense—but I don't know how to recreate it two thousand miles away from my nearest relatives. My attempts to do the seder myself with friends haven't turned out that well. I'm always grateful to be invited out for Passover—and not just because I don't have to cook. I like to be remembered, especially at holidays.

However, I've yet to feel at home at someone else's seder table. I think I know why Elijah (the prophet, for whom a place is set) never shows up. If the family I'm visiting is wonderful, I become envious and then annoyed with myself for feeling that way; and if there's a lot of tension at the table, I'd just as soon not be there.

Maybe there will be a spin-off to *Queen for a Day* called *Married for a Week* that will solve my problem. I could win the Grand Prize and be awarded a husband and children of my own for Passover week. I'd bring the kids into the kitchen and demonstrate how to grate the onions and potatoes as my mother and grandmother once showed me. I'd complain to the family about how hard I worked preparing the feast. It makes it all worthwhile if you can complain about it. But mostly I'd pass on what I still remember of the Passover traditions.

I long to be able to do that. It's what this holiday is all about. One reason singles feel shut out at Easter, Passover, Hanukkah or Christmas is that we can't pass on our heritage to anyone. We are caught in a double bind. Those times of the year when we experience the strongest pull to be Catholic or Jewish or Protestant in a public way, we are made to feel out of place. Any single who attends a seder or goes to Easter Mass is surely hit in the face with the extent to which these great religious celebrations are about family and children. Knowing that has been true for thousands of years doesn't make us feel any less estranged.

We need to realize this isn't just our problem. It's also the problem of organized religion, which has done little to develop a set of experiences that speak to the single life. It's no wonder that most people join a church or synagogue *only* after they have had children.

When seders are held at synagogues, singles are often put at tables by themselves. It's not too hard to imagine some "Yenta the matchmaker" working furiously behind the scenes. So much of what passes for singles activities among religious groups is really little more than trying to get people married off. There's got to be another way to make them feel they belong.

A Birthday Is No Time to Grow Up

I have an exaggerated sense of my birthday's importance, for which I blame my mother. She threw the most lavish parties for me—sit-down lunches for fifty screaming kids followed by puppet shows or treasure hunts and, as I grew older, elegant dinners for pre-pubescent boys and girls whose pre-sexual antics must have made her wish for the years when all my friends did was throw food.

After I left home, I received three birthday cards from my mother every year. One was signed with her name and the others with the names of my sister and brother, in case they forgot to send anything. There didn't seem to be any point in telling my mom I recognized her handwriting and, anyway, I liked getting all those cards. Now that she is gone, there aren't that many people left I can count on to remember my birthday.

The down side of being single and childless is that you aren't regenerating family members who are more or less obligated to pay attention to you on the anniversary of the day you were born, and can be made to feel guilty should they forget. I suspect that may be why singles make such a fuss about their own birthdays. We feel we have to alert everyone to the great day, lest in pass unheralded.

My single friends have parties for themselves or prevail on someone to do it for them. The main reason for the latter is that you start to feel a little silly about throwing a party for yourself year after year.

There is something distinctly childlike about these affairs, with their party favors and cakes decorated with birthday greetings. The birthday boy or girl—which is what he or she acts like—goes through the ritual of opening the presents, accompanied by extravagant oohs and aahs and, on occasion, even some sexual antics and throwing of food.

It may be that married people also celebrate their birthdays in this fashion, but I don't recall ever being invited to any of their parties (with the exception of a fortieth-birthday party, which is a milestone for everyone, married or single). I have, however, been asked to parties they give for their children.

I have a theory about all this. I think there is a limited amount of energy for the planning and execution of birthday parties, and that parents expend all of it on their kids, while singles expend it on themselves—becoming children again in the process. But why would we want to be children, even for a day? *Because your birthday is when you are the most susceptible to the feeling that nobody loves you, and therefore might want to retreat back to a time when you were secure in knowing you were loved.*

I become at least immature, if not downright childish, around my birthday. I drop a lot of hints that it is coming up (though I have never been as blatant as the friend who swiped my pocket calendar and wrote his birth date and shirt size under the appropriate day). I walk around on my birthday like I am queen for the day. I was once in New York on that date and decided I should lunch at one of those uptown restaurants where you have to know Jackie O. to get in. I sauntered in, said it was my birthday and got a table without a reservation.

An invitation to my birthday party is a command appearance. While I am not one to hold grudges, I remember everybody who didn't show up for one of my parties, going back for years. They don't often get asked back. This has nothing to do with presents, which I can take or leave. It has to do with people fussing over me.

Like most singles, I do fine every other day of the year without that. But on my birthday I feel I am entitled to special treatment, and I fear I will do something really childish, such as stomp my feet, if I don't get it.

Being Single These Days Is Hard Work

If there is any holiday that might make you think about work, it's Labor Day. And what I have been thinking is that single people have a complicated relationship with their workplaces.

I can't say that I work harder since I've been single, but my work habits are different. When I had a husband expecting me home (to, among other things, make dinner), I would leave the office at 5:30 p.m., no matter what. There was a clear separation between my work life and my other life. I thought of the latter as my real life, although, as it turned out, no part of it exists anymore, whereas I still get up every day and go to work—which is about as real as life gets.

By choice, I now go into the office later and stay later. I love to have the mornings to myself and not have to talk to anybody. To me, that is one of the best parts of living alone. Having been relieved of K.P. ,the time between 5:30 and 7:30 p.m. would be wasted anyway, so I am perfectly content spending it at my desk. I then have the rest of the evening to do anything I want.

But I find it harder to get away from work completely. It overlaps the other parts of my life more than it did when I was married. I don't hesitate to take on a weekend assignment or to stay at the office late if need be. Inevitably, the colleagues who are there with me are also single.

You don't catch people with families hanging around the office at night unless it's an emergency. That doesn't necessarily mean single people are workaholics. However, they may be guilty of stretching out a workload, perhaps without even realizing it, to escape dealing with the rest of their lives. I admit I've done this myself.

Your relationship to work depends on how seriously you work at being single. It takes a lot of energy to be dating, and that depletes the amount you have to give at the office. Dating can also be distracting, especially if you are the emotional type who is always falling in and out of love. You'll be staring into space when you should be staring into your computer, or whatever it is you are paid to stare into.

I remember a period right after my divorce when I couldn't concentrate on work because I was thinking about men or talking to them or talking about them to my girlfriends. I felt so guilty—that's Jewish guilt, not the Protestant work ethic—that I stayed late to make up for the time I frittered away.

(The Glenn Close character in the movie *Fatal Attraction* is an extreme example of this. She was supposed to be a hotshot book editor in New York, though I don't know how she could have gotten anything accomplished between harassing Michael Douglas on the phone and traipsing off to his office to do so in person.)

The latest complication for single employees—probably married ones, too, but that's not my concern—is the "office romance." According to a rash of articles, it is positively rampant. More than 80 percent of workers report some kind of "social-sexual" experience on their jobs, and 26.1 percent say they have had sex in their actual place of business.

That last figure gave me pause. I don't know what your office looks like, but mine is short on facilities for close encounters of that kind.

It is difficult enough to work when your romantic interest is on the other side of town. What must it be like with this person at the next desk? The articles imply that everyone is acting terribly mature and that office romances are not disrupting the workplace. The turmoil may not be visible, but it has to be going on in people's hearts and souls.

I worry about what happens at the end of the affair. Imagine having to face an ex-lover every day. Or do you think that person will conveniently quit on your behalf? I predict a lot of late hours at the office—not making love, but making up for the time that love takes.

WHAT FRIENDS ARE FOR

Everybody needs friends, but you especially need them when you're single. They fill in for a missing spouse and children. We depend on friends to hang out with, to cheer us on when good things happen and to comfort us in times of trouble.

It's easier in the '90s than it has ever been for men and women to be buddies. You can look to your buddy to give you the straight scoop on the opposite sex, as well as to escort you on those occasions when you need a date and have no one else to ask. When women want to talk, particularly about men, they turn to their female friends. These conversations go on forever, like a soap opera. Women analyze each other. They can be tough, but they have a way of seeing a friend's problems more clearly than she can.

In the throes of a romance, friendships may seem less important. But when your lover has left, your friends will still be there. That's what friends are for.

A Woman Needs Her Spare Man

It was my friend Lowell who came up with "designated hitter" to describe the position Mark plays in my life. I had called to ask if I could bring Mark to dinner at Lowell's house because the guy I was planning to go with would be out of town. I reminded Lowell that he had met Mark when he accompanied me to an office party at the last moment after my date had gotten sick.

"Right, Mark's the designated hitter," said Lowell, one of those sportswriters who is always seeing life as a metaphor for sports. (As any baseball fan knows, though it had to be explained to me, the designated hitter is the team member who bats for the pitcher because the pitcher can't do the job himself.)

I suppose that is the place I've assigned Mark in my lineup of men. Whoever the players are—and there have been substitutions over the years—Mark is always there to pinch-hit.

It's an ideal arrangement for both of us. I go out a lot, and, while I'm usually content on my own or with my girlfriend, there are some things, like formal parties and big-deal openings, where it's kind of nice to appear with a man. But men are not always reliable—which is why it helps to have a spare. Mark never seems to mind being second choice, and he is cool enough not to inquire about the date who canceled. He is happy to go with me anywhere, on an hour's notice, if he has no other plans.

Most often, he doesn't. Another reason our relationship works so well is that I'm a planner, and Mark is the hang-loose type who, as he puts it, waits to see what will turn up on any given night, such as a phone call from me.

Mark is the perfect escort. He is very funny and cute. He is also the only man I know who owns a tuxedo, so if the event is black tie, he gets called first. (The tux is an anomaly; his mother bought it for him ten years ago when Mark, who is a photographer of some note when he's not busy being my escort, was shooting an awards dinner in New York. He doesn't even own a suit; but that's O.K., because men with suits are a dime a dozen.)

We have a great time together. Since we have been friends forever, I can be myself around him. I don't have to be charming unless I feel like it, and after a hard day, I often don't.

I think every woman should have a designated hitter on her team. However, for this to happen, the two of you have to play by the same rules:

• You must be absolutely clear that you are just friends. If either one harbors any illusions of a romance, you're both going to strike out.

• If you are between boyfriends, the designated hitter might be promoted to a full-time position. But he needs to understand this is just temporary and pretty soon he will be back on the bench.

• He should play the field on his own. If he were to have a serious girlfriend, she might not want him on someone else's team.

It is on this last point that Mark and I have sometimes gotten into trouble. While he has become buddies with the men I go out with, I rarely like his women. It has occurred to me that I am too hard on them.

There was one woman named Anna, with whom Mark was so smitten he talked about their living together. One evening, Anna joined a bunch of us for dinner at a trattoria. She was a slow eater, or maybe it was that we all ate so fast. (When we're together, we tend to forget not to talk with our mouths full.) Anyway, while we were gulping down our zabaglione, Anna was still on the antipasto.

She and Mark broke up shortly afterwards. I don't think the meal had anything to do with it, though I did ask him rather pointedly if she always ate so slowly. To this day, if Mark and I are ordering dessert, I'll suddenly remember Anna and start to laugh. Mark, who laughs at almost anything, does not join in.

I realize that my inability to go all out for Mark's girlfriends may have something to do with a fear of losing him. I need my designated hitter. I don't want him going off and being a free agent or, even worse, retiring from the game.

Together, We Surely Have It All

For fourth-graders, Diane and I used to have awfully serious discussions about what we were going to be when we grew up.

Diane wanted to be a nurse or maybe even a doctor—a pretty lofty ambition for a girl back in 1954—and care for people in places like India and Armenia. I imagined myself a writer, probably because I kept getting A's on my class essays. (After writing that my pet peeve was always being assigned to the first row, first seat because my last name started with "B," I was banished to the back of the room—my first lesson in the power of the written word.)

Now, whenever I see Diane, who became a doctor and comes to San Francisco from time to time for medical conferences, we talk more about the past than the future. The last time we were together, we reminisced about the restaurant our mothers used to take us to that had a treasure chest from which we could choose one elaborately wrapped present, provided we had finished our lunch. The temptation was to grab the biggest box, but we learned that the best things sometimes came in small packages.

We laughed about when we were eleven and responded to an ad for a horror picture promising your money back if you were too scared to sit through it and were willing to stand in a "coward's corner" in the lobby for all to see.

Thinking we were pretty smart, we watched the entire other feature on the double bill before walking out on the scary movie.

Though we cowered in the corner as we were supposed to, our money was not refunded. That was the first time we realized that life isn't fair, and that we weren't as smart as we thought we were.

We wondered what had become of the kids we went to school with, like Nathan, who smashed a globe to pieces in geography and threw them out the window continent by continent, or Delba, who had the highest I.Q. of all of us but never had any boyfriends, so we couldn't really be jealous of her.

Staying up most of the night talking, just as we had once done at pajama parties, Diane and I confronted the possibility that we might now be a little jealous of each other. To me, Diane seemingly had it all: the career, the husband, the children—a boy and a girl—to make the picture perfect. When she told me about the hayride she was planning for her daughter's birthday, I longed for a child to plan a party for.

She, in turn, was in awe of the life I lead, which she has fantasized as being more glamorous than it is. The first day she was here, I took her to a ballet. Diane, who lives in a rural area more than three hundred miles from a major city, hadn't been to one in years. Putting on her big-city dress, she sighed, "I feel so grown up."

Yet compared to her, I felt like a child with no real responsibilities. She had a serious job; mine seemed like playing. She was saving to send her children to college; I was saving to send myself on another trip. When I talked to her about my latest romance, I think I must have sounded like a teenager in love.

Diane couldn't believe how quiet my apartment was, nor how neat and clean. It amazed her that things remained just where I'd left them. Her description of the commotion at her house, with kids and friends constantly in and out—probably intended to horrify me—sounded like fun. She told me she got up early some mornings just to have a few moments of silence. I told her I went out at night to escape the sounds of silence.

Diane envies my freedom, especially to travel. She would still like to be a doctor in an impoverished part of the world, but that sort of thing is hard to do with a family. I wouldn't mind having some kind of anchor to keep me in one place.

When Diane and I got around to talking about the future, it was with a sense of resignation. We were both basically happy with our lives, which was good, because changing them in any fundamental way wasn't as easy as it once was.

We used to think we could have everything we wanted, but have found choosing "this" usually means we can't have "that." We simply don't have as many options as we used to. That's one of the lessons of middle age. It's good to learn it with an old friend.

Men: The Talk of the Table

Jessica, Patti and I had caught up on our jobs, travels and the latest gossip when the dinner conversation turned to men. In the eighteen years we've been friends, over countless dinners, breakfasts, lunches and midnight phone calls, the conversation has somehow always turned to men. It may be a measure of our maturity that at least they're no longer the *first* thing we talk about.

There have been the men who broke our hearts; the ones whose hearts we broke; the ones we married; the ones we divorced. Now Jessica, happily remarried, listens when Patti and I bring up the subject of single men.

Talking about men, I have come to believe, is an integral part of dating them. Women friends validate the experience. It's a variation of the age-old question: If a tree falls in a forest and no one hears it, did it make a noise? If I go out and no one hears about it, did the date really happen?

My teenage diary is filled with fleeting references to Guy, Donny and Howie. However, Suzy, my confidante in those days, is mentioned on almost every page.

I would rush home from a date and immediately call her with news of the first kiss, the first serious necking and the first fight. I would cry to her when the romance came to an end. Suzy probably heard more than she cared to; but she was in no position to say anything, since I was listening to her go on about Mike, Jimmy and Hank.

As one who has been on both sides of men talk, I know how the game is played. You should never challenge your girlfriend in the heady, early days of a romance. Just listen and maybe throw in an occasional "Really?" when she tells you how terrific he is.

Women have a tendency to boast about the men they are seeing. It's not so different, I suspect, from the sexual boasting that men do with each other. Hyping a new beau, which I'm as guilty of as the next woman, is a way of showing off to your girlfriends. What you're really saying is, "I met this wonderful guy and eat your heart out, he's interested in me." So he becomes a little more wonderful than he really is, more successful, better-looking, smarter.

As sure as he starts out sounding like Superman, he's going to end up sounding like super-jerk. Once your girlfriend begins bad-mouthing him, don't be so unkind as to remind her of the praise she heaped on him. Simply agree. When *she* loves him, *you* love him. When *she* hates him, *you* hate him. That's what friends are for.

With the quick turnover in relationships these days, you may not even have a chance to meet the guy. Like a character in a novel, he'll exist only through description. But while the cast of male characters is constantly changing, women friends stay the same. Over the lifetime of a friendship, you will have hashed over lots of men together.

Jessica, Patti and I laugh about the turkeys we have gone out with. They remember my turkeys better than I do. What I remember is our conversations. In retrospect, they seem the best part.

Getting Older Brings Out the Vamp

Between the chicken soup and the pot roast, Barbara figured out what was going on with me. She had invited me over because, as hard as it was for me to admit it, I needed a friend. We were sitting around her kitchen table discussing my sudden desire to vamp every man I met.

"You know," she said, with a pause that would have cost ten bucks in therapy, "it could have to do with your birthday coming up."

Until she brought it up, I hadn't thought about my birthday, at least not consciously. I wasn't about to turn a milestone age or anything. I have a cavalier attitude about my age. I suspect the reason I'm so quick to volunteer it is that people seem surprised when I do. They tell me I don't look it.

Was it possible the prospect of turning forty-four bothered me more than I let on even to myself? Was I seeking affirmation from men that it didn't bother them? Or, better yet, that they had no idea I was that old? Yes, I thought, all of the above.

I've always taken my looks for granted. They are a part of who I am. I have good teeth, ugly toes, I talk too much and I'm pretty. I like it that men whistle at me; I liked it even during the women's movement when I wasn't supposed to. But I've been whistled at for so long, I hardly hear it anymore. If it stopped, would I suddenly become aware of the silence, as when the refrigerator abruptly stops humming? Women tell me the worst thing about getting older is the way men look past you, as if you weren't there. I dread that happening.

I get spooked by the song "Memory," which for some reason (the one Barbara came up with is as good as any) I have been listening to a lot lately. The part that really gets me is the plaintive "Touch me; it's so easy to leave me, all alone with the memory of my days in the sun." It makes me think I had better take advantage of the sunny days I have left.

I've considered I may be going through the basic midlife crisis, the sort that causes responsible men to leave their wives and run off with twenty-five-year-old secretaries. Lacking a twenty-five-year-old underling, I seem to be chasing something else: proof that I still have it.

My pattern in the past has been to be cautious about men I don't know very well. I have my feet planted firmly on the ground, at least at the beginning. After years of averting my eyes when I catch men looking at me, I find myself staring at them to see whether they'll stare back. When they do, I'm grateful. A guy in a pickup truck passed me the other morning and waved and honked his approval. I almost jumped out of my car and kissed him.

I used to make a thing of telling a man I was dating not to compliment me on my appearance. It seemed my other attributes should matter more. Now I can hardly wait to be flattered, and I don't mean about my mind. I have been reduced to asking for it. "Do you like my new dress?" I've heard myself ask on more than one occasion.

I adored being told by a younger man that I was not just "comely," but "very comely." I even looked the word up in the dictionary to prolong the praise. My younger man suggested I try "floating" for a change. I wasn't sure what he meant, but it sounded like fun.

I probably would have floated right through my birthday if Barbara hadn't brought me down. She told me that I'm being silly, that men will find me attractive for a long time to come, and that I don't need all their affirmation right now. She says I'll be having romances when I'm in a nursing home. Somehow I don't find that thought cheering.

A Lovely Lady Can't Hold Men

When Jean and I met for dinner, she had the latest scoop on Sara. The guy in Los Angeles—the one Sara was just sure was The One—had stood her up on their second date. We both had the same thought, but Jean got it out first: "What is it with Sara, anyway?"

In the six years we've all been friends, Sara has never had a serious relationship. She left San Francisco because she said there were no men in this town; now it seems there aren't any in Los Angeles, either. Jean and I don't understand why someone as lovely and accomplished as Sara can't find a man. It's especially baffling to us because we don't have that problem. When we're all out together, Sara, who looks like a blond Jacqueline Bisset, gets the stares. But we get the boyfriends.

The day after Jean left the guy she had been living with, she went to the movies by herself. She made a funny comment about the film to a guy a few seats away. He joked back, and they have been going out ever since. If she can find a boyfriend at a movie theater, why has Sara had such rotten luck up and down California?

Like Jean, I have had men walk into my life without even trying. I've come to feel I can practically will one to appear. This is the sort of thing Jean and I have talked about with each other, but never, ever, with Sara. It would be tacky to bring it up—like telling someone who has just declared bankruptcy that you have money to burn. However, we have chided Sara for thinking that her problem is meeting men. She meets them easily enough. It's what happens later that causes the angst.

Jean and I have been through the highs and lows with her so often, we can no longer get excited when she calls with news of the latest man. We know it will be a matter of weeks—or even days—before he stops calling or announces he has gone back to his former girlfriend. These guys can't all be jerks, as Sara insists. Some of the fault has got to be hers.

I suspect Sara is one of those people who has a hard time bonding with the opposite sex. She's great with women and collects girlfriends with an ease I admire. But around men, it's a different story. Her compulsive phone calls to her women friends to report every detail of every date seem to me symptomatic of the problem she has with men. She always sounds so uninvolved, as though she were reciting the plot of a soap opera.

This isn't my style. When I care about a man, I stop talking about him. It's too personal. My loyalty is to him. I can't believe he would want to be Topic A. I know Jean feels the same way, since I only hear about her boyfriends when she's breaking up with them.

Sara seems to look upon each potential boyfriend as a potential enemy. Even in the giddy early stages, she's prepared for the worst. He could turn out to be a jerk. Sure enough, he inevitably does.

I don't know how a romance can get off the ground without the feeling that the two of you are on the same side—if not friends yet, at least not enemies. Once that bonding occurs, the chances diminish that one person will drop out of sight with no explanation. You might still break up, but you'll know the reason. I'm talking about the ability to become intimate fast—and I don't mean jumping into bed on the first date. It could be that some people have an intimacy gene and others don't.

Jean and I have wondered whether relationships are easier for us because we have been married. We know what it is like to form the ultimate bond. (We also know what it's like to break it.) But that's the old chicken-and-egg argument. Our ability to get close to men could be the reason we got married in the first place.

Either way, it doesn't help our friend in Los Angeles or the many others like her. Sara is going to have to resolve her problem with men herself. When she finally does, Jean and I will know because we won't have to hear about it.

An Affair: To Have or Have Not?

On the same day, two friends—both in so-called committed relationships—took me aside and confessed they're thinking about having affairs. Their confessions were predictably tepid, given that nothing had happened, at least not yet. Nonetheless, I listened attentively while avoiding saying anything that could be construed as advice. Experience has taught me to stay out of other people's affairs—real or imagined.

Six months from now, I don't need Friend Number One screaming at me: "You told me to go ahead and sleep with Alvin. Well, not only did he turn out to be a jerk, but Haskell caught us together and left me."

Nor do I need to hear this tirade from Friend Number Two: "I listened to you and didn't call Zelda, and where did it get me? Dora and I broke up anyway, and now Zelda is with someone else when she ought to be with me."

Besides not wanting to be the fall gal, I didn't tell them what to do because I honestly don't know. While I believe it's immoral for married couples to be unfaithful, I'm not sure the same ethics should apply to singles who couple. The same definitions certainly don't apply. For instance, Webster tells us: "Adultery can be applied only to sexual intercourse between a married person and a partner other than his or her wife or husband." In other words, if you're not married, it's not adultery.

Singles talk about being in a "committed relationship," which is code for saying they don't play around. The very expression implies there are noncommitted relationships in which people do just that. You would never say you were in a committed marriage. All marriages are committed ones, at least in theory.

We need a new vocabulary just to be able to explain the complicated arrangements of modern love lives. We could also use our own code of ethics, or, short of that, an Eleventh Commandment: *Thou shalt not commit fornication.*

Because it hasn't been spelled out, most unmarried couples negotiate the fidelity issue. Usually, it is couched in terms of whether they will be allowed to see other people, but there is no mistaking what "see" really means. The person who has initiated the conversation is automatically suspect. He or she wouldn't be asking unless somebody was already lined up.

Here's one instance in which singles would be better off following the example of married folks and shutting up about their affairs, before as well as after. Open marriages turned out to be a disaster, and there's no reason why open relationships should fare any better. Nobody really wants to know the truth. The issue is your obligation to a person you profess to love. Do you owe it to him or her to remain faithful and, if so, for how long? That has become harder to answer since relationships are dragging on forever, longer even than marriages.

There are other difficult questions my two friends must be asking themselves:

• "I'm not married to Haskell/Dora, so what's stopping me from having an affair?"
• "Will I be able to get away with it?"
• "If not, can I bear to see Haskell/Dora hurt?"

The only encouragement I'll offer my confused friends is to go right on thinking about their affairs. There's nothing wrong with that. I'd even recommend it to married people.

I myself have had hundreds of fantasy affairs. I imagine what I would wear to a liaison, where we would go—well, you get the picture. Thinking about an affair, I've found, is often the best part.

While my friends are thinking, I hope they give a little thought to *why* they feel tempted to stray. It could be that other people are looking good to them because they want out of the relationship they're in. If that's the case, maybe instead of taking a lover, they should take a breather. Trial separations are a lot simpler when you're not married.

I'd better stop there. This is starting to sound like advice.

Heading Off Dangerous Attractions

It's not supposed to happen, but sometimes it does. You're introduced to your best buddy's girlfriend and there's a flutter, a spark—the thing that is not supposed to happen. If you're the right kind of person, you'll feel guilty; if you're human, you can't help but feel titillated, too.

These are dangerous attractions, to be sure. But it's not surprising they occur when you consider that single people go through relationships a lot faster than they go through friendships. The more of your friends' dates you meet, the greater the likelihood one of them will arouse feelings you would just as soon not have.

I believe there would be more dangerous attractions if it weren't for an "off" button that gets automatically activated around people who are not available. I can't show it to you on an anatomy chart, but I'm convinced such a button exists. The one time I *was* seriously attracted to a friend's beau, I didn't realize he was the new man in her life until it was too late to switch off my button. (For all she had told me about him, she had neglected to mention his last name.)

I met him at a business luncheon during a period when I was between men. We chatted, and I flirted and I swear he did, too—though I never asked him whether the attraction was mutual, because once I figured out who he was, I didn't want to know. After that, whenever I would see this man with my girlfriend, I would try to avoid them. She thought I just didn't like him. How could I tell her I liked him too much?

One evening, as we were all leaving a restaurant together, I impulsively kissed him good-bye. That had the unexpected though certainly welcome effect of diffusing my feelings. Still, I was relieved when he took a job in another city.

Talk about guilt. To this day, I haven't said a word about any of this to my friend. Yet I also tell myself I have nothing to feel guilty about. I didn't *do* anything.

I did not break the second commandment of friendship: Thou shalt not fool around with thy friends' dates. (The first commandment is to always be there in times of need.)

Being attracted to someone in itself isn't wrong. It's pretty much out of your control anyway. Feelings are a natural outpouring as opposed to, say, an oil spill. However, it is wrong to act on those feelings. It's an awful thing to do to a friend, the ultimate betrayal. If a dangerous attraction is pursued, it will almost surely be fatal to your friendship.

I once taught with two women—I'll call them Peg and Meg—who were as close as sisters until Peg's boyfriend left her and began dating Meg. Peg was convinced their romance had started when she was still with this man. (I'm not so sure, though I do think the seeds were planted and encouraged to grow.) She felt much more betrayed by her girlfriend than her ex and never spoke to her again—not even after Meg was also jilted. "I don't see how I could ever trust her again," Peg said.

Dangerous attractions can be terribly seductive, in part because they are so illicit. But far more satisfying is the mastery that comes with having some control over your desires and not letting them control you.

However, as my experience shows, it's not obvious what to do about a dangerous attraction, even after you've decided to do nothing. I don't believe everybody should sit down and talk about it. There's no reason for the third party ever to be involved. He or she would only be hurt by the revelation of an attraction, however innocent, between the other two.

That leaves the question of whether those two should admit how they feel and get the whole thing out in the open in the hope that that will dissipate it. But what if it turns out the attraction isn't mutual? One person will probably walk away feeling pretty silly. Even if it is mutual, some things are better left unsaid.

The best idea may be to shut up about your feelings and hope they go away and that the next time your friend falls for someone, your "off" button activates properly.

Friendship Is a Do-It-Yourself Undertaking

In the "What Will They Think of Next?" category is a new service that brings people together not for purposes of romance, but friendship. Send in fifty dollars and you receive a list of twenty-five would-be friends screened for you by the service. That breaks down to two bucks per buddy.

I find it incredible and kind of sad that anyone would be reduced to finding friends this way. Friendships are so personal, how could they possibly be entrusted to a mail-order business?

I feel the same way about those who depend on outside sources to find dates for them or, for the really desperate, mail-order brides. Professional matchmakers don't come cheap, and I can't buy the notion that they know more about what you want than you do. As far as I'm concerned, the personals are such a cold way to meet someone, they should be called the "impersonals." The problem with these attempts to hook up people is that they're so contrived. In my experience, the best friendships as well as the best relationships just happen.

My first best friend was Dorene Sohr. We met in the playground on the first day of first grade when I fell down and skinned my knee—I was always skinning my knees and have the scars to show for it—and she took it upon herself to comfort me. No decision was made that we would be friends. We just started talking and didn't stop until two years later, when her family whisked her away to someplace called the suburbs, which to a city girl like me whose mother didn't drive might as well have been Siberia. I never saw Dorene again, but much of what I know about being close to another person came out of that primal friendship.

I've sought to recreate the feeling I always had with her of being at a movable pajama party—a little giddy from staying up too late and free to be completely myself with the confidence that nothing I could say would make Dorene like me any less. This was more difficult after I became interested in boys. *Everything* was more difficult after I became interested in boys.

However, I've come to believe that a relationship is simply a close friendship with sex thrown in. (Yes, I am aware that can be a heavy weight.) You can extrapolate what you learn from a friendship to the other kind of "ship" you find yourself in, beginning with:

• Trust your instincts. I've never wound up friends with anyone I didn't immediately like. Yet singles are continually being admonished to give their date a chance, that he or she will grow on you after a while. I doubt it. The chemistry is either there or it isn't.

• You've got to get out there to meet anyone. Admittedly, it's not as easy as it was in grade school, when we were all thrown into the same playground together. But if you go about your life—and that means getting out of the house—sooner or later someone will walk into it you want to be friends with, or maybe more than friends.

• It doesn't matter who makes the first move—or the second or the third. Friends don't waste any time worrying whether the other one is going to call. I've begun to think this is a bogus issue in dating, too. When a relationship is right, you don't wait for the phone to ring—because you know where you stand.

• Being together should be fun—not work. You wouldn't stay in a friendship you had to work at to make enjoyable. That just happens, like the movable pajama party I had with Dorene. Why do couples think they have to work at their relationships? If it's too much work, something's wrong.

• Forget the discussions about what you mean to each other and where it's all headed. Friends don't need reassurance that their friendship is real. Those heavy-duty talks about your "relationship" can be oppressive.

• Friendships/relationships are meant to be. This gets back to my pet theory that fate has a big hand in the people we go through life with. This mystical selection process should be left alone, not interfered with by services claiming to find friends or lovers for you.

Friendships Don't Always Last Forever

Sending out Christmas cards makes me a little sad. As I go through my address book, names pop out at me of friends I never see anymore. I don't mean people who live on the other coast; I mean people who live on the other block.

I could claim the usual excuses for letting these friendships lapse. I seem to always have something more pressing to do. I am not good about calling just to stay in touch. (It's not as easy as the phone company would have us believe.) I don't know what to say to someone I haven't spoken to in months, or years. ("Hi, remember me? I used to be your friend.")

These excuses make me feel even worse because they imply I am to blame. If I weren't so busy or if I were better about picking up a phone, my friendships might all still be intact. But maybe they're not meant to be. Maybe there's a reason I'm not dialing those numbers. Maybe I have nothing to feel guilty about.

While we can accept the fact that most romantic relationships come to an end, there is no similar resolution for a friendship that has lost its raison d'être. After one wrenching evening, a boyfriend is no longer a boyfriend. But friends don't meet for a drink and say, "Listen, this just isn't working out."

Yet the same complicated emotions that bring people together as lovers also bring them together as friends. You need something from this other person—whether it be intimacy or companionship or simply someone with whom to hang out—and can give him or her something in return. Then, for whatever reason, your needs change. And there you are, stuck with the shell of a friendship and a name in an address book and a lingering feeling you are supposed to be friends forever—as if you had pricked each other with a needle just as you did when you were kids and swore eternal friendship over co-mingled blood.

It is especially hard to let go when you have been through an intense experience together. For instance, I have this friend named Laura. (Note that I say "have," though we haven't talked in about two years.) She was the person in whom I confided when my marriage was falling apart. I went through the giddy early stages of being single with her as well. We did the singles bars and parties together. (I was with Laura the night my mother, frantic because there was no answer at my house at 3:00 a.m., called my ex-husband to ask whether he knew where I was.)

The easy explanation of what happened to our friendship is that Laura got married and, not long after, had a child. She became a turf person: If I wanted to see her, I had to go over to her house. However, we might have stayed close if I hadn't also changed during that period. Laura loves to chat, and I lost my taste for it. I no longer reported my every thought to her. I must have sounded impatient when she went on and on about nothing, because eventually she stopped calling.

I find I have many more male friends than I used to, and I wonder whether my giving up chatting has anything to do with it. Men are not good at chitchat, and they like listening to it even less.

I don't need friends the way I did right after my divorce, when I looked to them as spouse substitutes. I am far more sufficient unto myself. I don't need a friend to confide in or gossip with or accompany me around town. I do need a friend I can count on to be there, should I ever need him or her, and I am lucky to have a half-dozen friends like this. I like to think that's the kind of friend I am, too.

So often when I am mulling over an idea, I will pick up a book or go to a play or movie that turns out to be about the very same thing. In one case, it was *Tequila Sunrise*, a surprisingly touching story for a film ostensibly about a drug bust, of two buddies who have overstayed their friendship. One of them questions why we think friendships should last forever. "You'd like them to," he says, "but sometimes they wear out, like everything else. They're like tires; pretty soon you're riding around on nothing but air."

Now, if I could just be as realistic as he is and erase all my run-down friendships—at least from my address book, if not from my memory.

NO FEAR OF
FLYING

I

t's a leap of faith comparable to getting on a plane to believe you will be perfectly safe while roaming the world alone. But trust me, you will, provided you plan your trips carefully and use some common sense.

Singles don't appreciate fully the freedom they have to go anywhere they want. You'll see places differently on your own. In Paris, for instance, you'll spend less time eating—that sumptuous food doesn't taste quite as good at a table for one—and more time admiring the city's architecture and great art museums.

Women traveling alone should be wary of the attention they are sure to receive from men. The Italians are the worst. They seem to think you've come to their country looking for them. But the good news is that if you ignore them, they will go away. You might be able to convince one of these pesky natives to show you around—no strings attached—but you really have to be fearless to pull this off.

Solo Travel Is the Ultimate Freedom

I have to make a decision soon about where in the world I want to go next year. The vacation schedule is about to be passed around at work, and before I sign up for a particular month, I really should have a destination in mind. April in Paris would be swell; April in the Yukon wouldn't be so hot.

I get out my globe and give it a few spins for inspiration. India, Thailand and Malaysia go twirling by, and I wonder what they would be like in April. I love having the whole world in my hands. It reinforces my conviction that the world is mine to roam. Eventually, I plan to see all of it. The only question is: In what order?

Now that I travel alone, I can go wherever I want whenever I want, without consulting anyone. If that isn't the ultimate liberation, I don't know what is. During the twelve years I was married to a psychiatrist, I had to go away in August because shrinks always go away in August. "Where do they all go?" a neurotic Woody Allen character (is there any other kind?) once asked. I know the answer firsthand. They go to meetings with other shrinks and pontificate on the art of shrinking while their wives go shopping.

I wonder whether singles appreciate their freedom to travel at will—no waiting for the kids to get out of school, no accommodating a spouse's idiosyncratic travel habits. It's puzzling to me when friends don't take advantage of this opportunity. They complain about not having anyone to go with, as if the world itself weren't company enough.

The hang-up usually isn't lack of money. Singles have more

disposable income than most other people. Besides, traveling by yourself abroad is relatively cheap. A single room goes for half the price of a double almost everywhere except in the States, where for some reason the rates are about the same. The real hang-ups are lack of imagination and lack of courage. We all need a little push to go out into the world.

I think of the sparrow that got trapped in the canopy outside my apartment building. The poor creature flew back and forth furiously, unaware that anything existed beyond its tiny universe until someone from the Humane Society set it free.

It's a leap of faith to believe you're as safe anywhere as you are in your own tiny universe. That doesn't mean that harm can't come to you, just that it is no more likely to befall you in Bath than in your bathtub. I didn't make that leap until five years ago, when I spent a summer alone in Europe.

I clipped a map out of an airlines magazine (well, I couldn't very well take my globe with me), and when I felt like moving on, I studied the map to decide where to go next. It was an incredible high to realize how easy it was to get around and how well I did on my own. I've stayed in touch with many of the people whose paths crossed mine that summer. This was networking on an international scale. When I was in New Zealand recently, I had dinner at the home of a retired Red Cross nurse I met on a train in Wales.

As adventurous as I have become, I still have to fight the temptation to keep returning to spots I know and love. I compromise by combining someplace known with someplace new—a stopover in London on my way to the Middle East, for instance.

China is tempting for my next trip. To lure tourists, the country has gone on sale, and I have a hard time resisting a sale. However, it doesn't seem a politically correct choice. On the other hand, the Soviet Union is quite politically correct. And I have a free ticket as far as Germany. (Another advantage of traveling solo is that when you accumulate enough mileage for two free tickets, you get to use both of them.)

I could do a "Roots" journey: ride a train through Poland and see where my mother's family was from, and then go into Russia, where my father was born. I've taken the first step toward making this trip a reality. I've started a file folder. It says, "Russia 1990." Eventually I plan to have the whole world filed away.

Paris Itself Is Enough Company

Paris is well known as a city for lovers. But unless you have spent time there alone, as I have, you might not realize it is also a city for loners. Its boulevards, gardens and parks seem designed for that most solitary of activities: walking. (Whenever Greta Garbo, the original loner, was surreptitiously photographed, the picture was always of her walking alone.)

Of course, one can take a walk with a companion. But then it becomes something else: a chat or, in the case of couples I saw smooching while strolling hand in hand along the Seine, foreplay.

Unlike Americans, Parisians don't seem self-conscious going to a movie or concert or anywhere else alone. They are their usual haughty selves. Dining solo is also no big deal. The natives do it all the time, often bringing a newspaper or book along for company. Then, too, brasseries actually have tables for one. (In the States, you are invariably seated at a table for four and sit there and cringe while the waiter makes a fuss about removing the extra service.) The tables in Paris are sensibly arranged in a row along a wall, so you are shoulder-to-shoulder with other singles looking at the action in the center of the room, instead of into someone's plate.

The French *savoir faire* made it easy for me to do Paris by myself. Of all the solo trips I have taken, this one was the most successful in the sense of feeling completely at ease.

There has been a definite progression in my travels. In the beginning, when I was newly divorced, it was enough just knowing I could handle the logistics of a trip myself. I took pleasure in being able to figure out the currency and how to get from Point A to Point B, whether the points were streets or cities or countries. Next, I went through an assertive phase when I demanded the same treatment as couples. I recall making a terrible fuss in a restaurant in Edinburgh because the maître d' had given the booth that should have been mine to a party of two.

Now when I travel, I want simply to "be"—and one can simply "be" in Paris better than anywhere else in the world. With invisible skywriting, the city appears to extend an open invitation. "Enjoy me," it says, "any way you want."

Having been there before in the company of men, I can compare those times with how I experienced Paris alone. For one thing, I spent less time eating and thinking about eating. Instead of devouring five-course dinners (after first poring through guidebooks with my mate to select the perfect restaurant), I went to hear some music or took in a film in the evening. The French are mad for American movies, and seeing one with them makes you somehow view it differently.

I also stayed late at museums. Most are open at least one night a week until 10:00 p.m. and become virtually deserted around that hour. I had the *Mona Lisa* to myself for a full fifteen minutes. I have never understood how you can look at a painting with someone else, anyway. How could two people possibly be so much in tandem that they would want to spend the same amount of time staring at a Picasso or a Monet?

There were works of art so wonderful I was relieved not to have to share my perceptions with anyone. I didn't want to have to explain how moved I was by Michelangelo's *Slaves* in the basement of the Louvre. (Reading Henry Adams' book about Chartres on my way to that great medieval cathedral outside Paris, I came across this line: "If you want to know what churches were made for, come down here on some great festival of the Virgin, and give yourself up to it, but come alone! That kind of knowledge cannot be taught and can seldom be shared.")

Sure, there were experiences I would have liked to share with someone, and other things I missed out on altogether because I was alone. It would have been nice having someone to smooch with along the Seine. But I didn't feel sad seeing all that *amour*. I rather liked it; it seemed very French. I've come back from Paris with no snapshots but with a lot of memories. I am content to be alone with them.

The Worst Thing About Italy Is the Men

The first night I was in Rome, I have to admit I found the attention from Italian men kind of flattering. I had gotten off one of those endless transcontinental flights, stopped at my hotel just long enough to drop off my bags and dashed over to the Spanish Steps so I would feel I was really there. Immediately, I had men come up to me and say, "*Bella, bella*," or make an appreciative clucking sound. Being in a stupor brought on by jet lag and still wearing the clothes I had on the day before, their reaction made me think that maybe I didn't look as undesirable as I felt.

However, I soon tired of the aggressive males who chased me across Italy like Hannibal's army. I have never been the sort of woman who gets insulted when strange men whistle at her. I've always found it rather nice. But the persistent comments and leering looks from Italians—ranging in age from young enough to be my son to old enough to be my grandfather— brought out the feminist in me. "How dare they?" I thought, although not having the language or the energy to get into a fight, I said nothing.

I tried ignoring them—a tactic that has worked with pesky men all over the world—but they wouldn't take the hint. It is the arrogance of Italian men that they can't quite believe a woman wouldn't be interested in them. It is also arrogance that they go right on staring, even if they are in the company of their wives.

I saw men lurking in train stations as if they were about to pounce on me and other men followed me down cobblestone streets and through open markets. I took a perverse pleasure in giving them the slip, ducking into an alleyway or a shop. I blame the men of Italy for my buying more in their country than I'd ever intended to.

One evening in Florence, I started running to get away from one of these turkeys who had invited me to have dinner with him, and ran smack into another one making the same offer. I had to laugh, which he took to mean "Yes," so I ran away from him too.

Men honked at me from behind the wheels of Italian sports cars. It was hard enough being a pedestrian in Italy, where the sidewalks as well as the streets seem to belong to motorists, without having to listen to those horns. I didn't know if a driver was honking at me because he liked my legs or because he was about to run me over.

Usually in foreign countries, I smile a lot, which is what you do when you don't speak the language. But on this trip, I hardly smiled at all, afraid that any sign of friendliness would be misinterpreted. I became suspicious of every male I met—as it turned out, with good cause.

At Pompeii, a guard let me leave the grounds to take a cappuccino break, assuring me I would be allowed back in without having to pay again. When I returned, he took my ticket—and my hand along with it. The porter at the hotel where I was staying in Sorrento pointed out a spectacular view from the terrace of the Bay of Naples. As I was admiring it, he practically insisted I go out with him.

I wonder what any of these guys would have done had I accepted, though I wasn't curious enough to try to find out. I have heard Italian men are all talk. Their advances scarcely made me feel as if I were irresistible. I couldn't even take them personally. Half the time it was so dark, they wouldn't have been able to see what I looked like before their come-ons.

I think they behave that way almost instinctively, because they grew up believing that's how Italian men are supposed to act. They have a reputation to live up to. I also suspect they don't quite know what to make of a woman traveling alone. Whatever their motivation, this tourist didn't appreciate being harassed for three weeks. It detracted from what should have been a perfect trip.

And on my last night in Italy, I confirmed what I had already suspected: Italian men are no gentlemen. I arrived at the Rome train station in a driving rain with two suitcases and a shopping bag full of my purchases. There was no cab in sight. I ended up walking for blocks, and not a single man offered to help. All they wanted to do was look.

Australia's Passive Men Ignore Ladies

Single women who complain about how hard it is to meet men in the United States should spend a few weeks in Australia, as I have. It is a country where women wait to be asked out—which means they spend a lot of time waiting. Aussie males seem to prefer the company of their male mates to the company of women.

Tracking men down isn't hard. They can be found at any pub, dressed in the Aussie uniform: a singlet and short shorts. (I suspect the scanty attire is to show off their tattoos.) Getting their attention is the hard part. They knock down huge mugs of beer—Foster's Lager, to be precise—while watching cricket or soccer or anything else that happens to be on TV. Nothing distracts them—certainly not the appearance of a woman. I had the feeling I could have done a striptease in the middle of the barroom floor, and not one man would have looked up.

I could take being ignored, knowing that I would soon be flying home. But I wondered how the women of Australia put up with it.

The first woman I asked, whom I noticed (even if none of the men did) sitting with her girlfriend in a Sydney pub, said she no longer expected to be approached, so she wasn't disappointed. If a man deigned to speak to her, he waited until the bar was about to close. "That way, he would only have to buy me one drink," she said.

She straightened me out on one point. Aussies actually do look at women, it's just that it happens very fast. The highest compliment they pay a woman is to mutter under their breath to their mate, "She's all right," which they slur together as if it were one word. Their laid-back attitude, which made Paul Hogan famous, makes the women I talked to furious. They accused their countrymen of being "on a macho trip," "bad-mannered" and "bad communicators." "They all speak out of the side of their mouths, like bad ventriloquists," one woman said indignantly.

Berwyn, a forty-three-year-old divorcée who is considering moving to the States just to get away from Aussie men, told about having one to dinner. She spent most of the day preparing a chicken dish, which he scarfed up as if he hadn't seen food in days. Then he announced he was sleepy. Before she had a chance to respond, "He was snoring his bloody head off on my sofa," she said. "I didn't want to be his mother and say, 'Wake up now. Mum will get you a cup of tea.' So I just said rather loudly, You have to leave now.'"

In the interest of fairness, I thought I better hear from some men, but realized it would be hopeless trying to get their attention at a corner pub. If I were in San Francisco and I wanted to talk to single men, I would go to a singles bar. However, trying to find one in Australia, even in supposedly sophisticated Sydney, wasn't easy.

The Aussies are still under the British influence to the extent that they think the proper place to meet is in a mutual friend's front parlor. This quaint tradition, on top of the indifference of Australian men, helps to explain why so many single women are frustrated.

Somebody finally tipped me off about Sheila's, a singles bar in North Sydney. I knew I had come to the right place when I saw the coasters. They said, "If you want to meet a friend, leave me this side up." The action was pretty slow that night, and I had no trouble finding a table of men eager to defend the reputation of the Aussie male.

First of all, they didn't see anything wrong with going to a pub to be with their mates and watch a cricket match. They compared it to the way women go to fashion shows with their girlfriends. "They wouldn't want a man distracting them from the clothes, now, would they?"

Peter, a twenty-eight-year-old bank clerk who expects to be married by thirty, though he has never had a serious relationship with a woman, said that if Australian men appear standoffish, it is because they are shy. "Like if I meet a girl I think is fantastic, I don't know what to say to her. I'm afraid of being rejected." His solution is not to say anything. He probably does that over a Foster's Lager with his mates.

Turning "Come-Ons" into Guided Tours

American women have a reputation for being fast. That's the rationale I've heard from men all over the world for their lurid looks and propositions. One does not have to understand the language to get their drift. I repeated this to my nineteen-year-old niece, Marcy, when she couldn't help noticing the way the two of us were being eyed on our travels through Israel. While I could explain the attention we were getting, I was torn on how to advise her to handle it.

Of course I knew what I should tell her: Ignore all those rogues. I've learned from experience this is the only tactic that works. If you try to answer them or defend your honor, they think you want to play.

The silent treatment was tailor-made for Israeli men, who, unlike Italians and Greeks, do know how to take no for an answer. Their manner of hustling women is to sneak up behind them on the street and whisper an invitation in their ear. If they get no response, they walk right on by. It's as if, living in a country that is always on the brink of war, they don't have a lot of time to waste.

Sometimes, though—and this is what I couldn't find the words to say to my niece—you might want to respond. It's one way to meet the natives and learn something about the place you're visiting. After all, you can't count on women or children to take the initiative to get to know you. However, to pull this off, you have to have good instincts about men and know how to deflect their amorous advances. Obviously, you are not going to strike up a conversation with a man who has just asked you to go to bed with him. But if the invitation is less blatant—say, for a drink—and if other people are around so you feel safe, you might consider hearing him out.

What you have to do is make him see you as a person, not just another loose American woman. I make a point of mentioning to him my boyfriend back home, whether or not I happen to have one. That's the only reason for rejection that men seem to understand. Then I bombard the fellow with questions about what I should see and do in his town. If he takes any pride in where he lives, he will metamorphose from would-be lover to tour guide.

I've had some wonderful times with men who may originally have had a different sort of time in mind. A Belgian I met on a street in Brussels ended up taking me around the university town of Louvain, where he had gone to school. An American living in Madrid escorted me to the best flamenco clubs in his adopted city. And a Greek working at the hotel where I was staying showed me a view of the Acropolis that wasn't in any of the guidebooks.

But somehow I didn't think Marcy's mother, my sister, would want me guiding her to such adventures, innocent as they were. On my travels with my niece, I was cast in the Maggie Smith role in *A Room with a View*, though I hardly felt old enough or chaste enough for it.

Not having made my opinion known, I was delighted when Marcy came back from an afternoon in the Old City in Jerusalem and told me about the young Israeli she had met there. He had asked her to lunch, and there was something about his face that made her accept. Afterward, he walked her all around the Arab and the Jewish Quarters, introducing her to his friends in both places. For the first time, she said, she had a sense of what it was like to live in Israel.

You know, Marcy said, she didn't think there was anything wrong with taking a walk with a man she met on a trip. But she would never go up to his room. Her aunt, the singles columnist, couldn't have put it any better.

Romance Is Rosier on Vacation

Once, on a vacation in Aspen, my friend Patti became smitten with a lanky skier named Karl. They had one of those magical first encounters, their eyes meeting across a crowded bar. His were a gorgeous blue, and he had just a touch of gray in his hair, so he looked dignified without looking old. The two were inseparable for a week. They skied together, dined at the best restaurants together, drank French wine together.

As soon as Patti got back to San Francisco, Karl was on the phone from Michigan wanting to know when he was going to see her again. But the Karl who came to visit three months later was not the Karl whom Patti remembered—or the one she had talked so much about. The big spender, who had bragged about his thousand-dollar-a-week condo in Aspen, arrived on a bus because it was cheaper to fly to Sacramento. His hair had gotten grayer, and his eyes were less blue.

The great raconteur was tongue-tied around Patti's friends. The guy who had looked so cute in a ski outfit appeared out of place in a polyester leisure suit. The wine connoisseur turned out to prefer beer.

After Patti had seen him off at the bus station, she called our friend Jessica for a postmortem. "Well," Jessica said, sagely, "I guess he just didn't transplant."

Most vacation romances don't transplant. They are very fragile things and are better off left in their place of origin. That way, you can look back on them fondly. To remove them to another setting is likely to kill not just the romance, but the memory too.

210

A lot of us, however, aren't content to leave well enough alone. If it was wonderful once, we reason, it can be wonderful again. We fantasize that this person we hardly know will fit right into our real life. It's no wonder that he or she is almost never the same. People aren't themselves on holiday. Given three days or a week in an exotic place, they feel free to act out any role they want. Timid types become uninhabited; cautious types go wild. In more real surroundings, the facade is harder to keep up.

Karl obviously had been acting the part of the big spender. (He'd saved his money for a year, Patti later found out, in order to play it to the hilt.) Normally, Patti would not have been impressed by being wined and dined. But on a trip, she found it irresistible.

On one of my vacations, I was totally charmed by an expatriate American who was living in Madrid. In his quest to seem European, he had changed his name from Lou to Luigi. I loved that he knew the best places to go for tapas and flamenco. Sitting in a café late at night, I found myself nodding my head a lot as he went on and on about what was wrong with the United States. He was so intense and, I thought, terribly bright. I wasn't prepared to renounce my citizenship, but I certainly wanted to see him again.

In the year that we exchanged letters, my fantasies got the best of me. I imagined us wandering through Europe together, like two characters out of a Henry James novel. One fantasy seemed to be coming true when we arranged a rendezvous in Paris.

Luigi didn't transplant. He no longer seemed bright, just bored. Paris didn't excite him. I didn't excite him. Nothing excited him. When I suggested we go to a Renoir exhibit, he told me he hated Renoir. How could anyone hate Renoir? During our last conversation, he accused me of being happy all the time—as if that were a character flaw.

O.K., so the guy was a loser. But why hadn't I seen that in Madrid? Because I was swept up by this notion of myself as a woman of the world. That was my part. His was this man who could teach me things. In a different setting, it became apparent that there was nothing I wanted to learn from him. I should have been content with the memory of Madrid. Now when I think of Luigi, I'll remember Paris.

REEL SINGLE LIFE

T

Movies are the literature of the twentieth century. They do more than tell us about the way we live. They show us.

What they have shown us about single life is pretty much the way it is, Hollywood glitz aside. There have been movies about singles bars, romances between older women and younger men, the heartbreak of breaking up and the panic among women who fear they may never meet Mr. Right. In deference to the AIDS scare, movies briefly avoided any suggestion of casual sex. Even James Bond became monogamous. But sex made a comeback in such trendy films as *Sea of Love* and *Fatal Attraction*. *Broadcast News*

215

examined whether a man's morals mattered and decided they did.

Love and romance have been a staple of the movies for a long time. Through the miracle of video, you can see for yourself how Hollywood has treated the subject over the years.

A Dozen Films Starring Your Life

How would you like a front-row-center seat for an entire film festival? I'm not talking Cannes. I'm not talking the New York or San Francisco festivals. I'm talking the first annual Singles Film Festival taking place right in your living room.

With a VCR and a catalog from your neighborhood video shop, it's easy to put on such a festival. You can be the program director, master of ceremonies and guest of honor. In keeping with the theme, though, you should watch all the movies by yourself and make your own popcorn during intermission. There are a surprising number of films about singles to choose from— going back more than fifty years to *Design for Living* starring Miriam Hopkins as a liberated lady with both Gary Cooper and Fredric March as her lovers.

Hollywood has tried to keep up with the singles trends. There have been movies about singles bars, free love, homosexual love, love between older women and younger men and the heartbreak and heartburn at the end of love. What there *hasn't* been, to the best of my recollection, is a movie about people who enjoy being single. The characters all seem to be desperately seeking anyone— and, by the last frame, they've usually found him or her.

Steve Martin in *The Lonely Guy* and Albert Brooks in *Modern Romance* were so miserable without a woman that you could hardly wait for those movies to end, so you could stop worrying about them. Audrey Hepburn was the quintessential party girl in *Breakfast at Tiffany's*, but she was constantly on the lookout for a rich husband. Jill Clayburgh found some happiness in *An Unmarried Woman*, but she had Alan Bates to help her through the rough times—which seems like cheating.

Here are the movies I would show at my Singles Film Festival. If you don't agree, put on your own festival.

• *How to Marry a Millionaire*, 1953, with Marilyn Monroe, Lauren Bacall and Betty Grable. A trio of luscious fortune hunters set a trap for a millionaire. If that is your goal in life, you'll pick up lots of helpful tips—though it might help more if you looked like one of the above. This film was made pre–women's liberation, yet hardly seems dated.

• *Marty*, 1955, with Ernest Borgnine and Betsy Blair. Before computer dating services and health clubs, a homely butcher and a shy schoolteacher find each other at a public dance hall. Marty's endless conversations with his buddy about how to spend another dateless Saturday night—"I don't know, Marty? What do you want to do?"—could have been written by Woody Allen.

• *Breakfast at Tiffany's*, 1961, with Audrey Hepburn and George Peppard. A deliciously amoral tale of the New York single life, circa late 1950s, though it cops out with an improbable happy ending. Hepburn is living off handouts from wealthy suitors, while Peppard, a down-on-his-luck writer, is being kept by a very rich, older woman. The big question, when they end up together, is: Who's going to support them?

• *Love with the Proper Stranger*, 1964, with Natalie Wood and Steve McQueen. Wood gets pregnant after a one-night stand with McQueen and spends most of the movie trying to convince him of his responsibility to do something about it. This may have been the first film to acknowledge that one-night stands were becoming commonplace and that even nice girls were doing it.

• *John and Mary*, 1969, with Dustin Hoffman and Mia Farrow. Hollywood discovers singles bars just a few years after everybody else. Hoffman picks up Farrow, takes her home with him and finds out her name a few nights later. The studio billed this one as a "story of today which starts with sex and ends with love." Ah, those were the good old days!

• *Carnal Knowledge*, 1971, with Jack Nicholson, Art Garfunkel,

Ann-Margret and Candice Bergen. Sex is all the men in this movie have on their mind—which isn't necessarily bad, though it can get tiresome. Worth seeing for Ann-Margret's stunning performance as a voluptuous redhead with marriage and not much else on her mind.

• *Annie Hall*, 1977, with Woody Allen and Diane Keaton. Still the smartest movie ever made about falling into and out of love. It's obvious that Allen and Keaton have been there together, but the awkwardness of their first few dates rings so true that Allen could have been filming your romance or mine.

• *An Unmarried Woman*, 1978, with Jill Clayburgh and Alan Bates. A serious look at what happens to a woman trying not to fall apart just because her marriage has. I could do without the therapy scenes, and her women's group ought to be gagged, but Clayburgh is quite convincing, especially as she discovers that sex with the proper stranger can be fun.

• *Moment by Moment*, 1978, with John Travolta and Lily Tomlin. Their careers almost didn't survive the devastating reviews of this film. But in retrospect its story of an affair between a forty-year-old divorcee and a nineteen-year-old parking lot attendant may simply have been ahead of its time. It has one line that a lot of women could have written. When Travolta tells her he's tired of cheap sex, Tomlin replies: "Really, I've never tried it. It sounds pretty good to me."

• *Modern Romance*, 1981, with Albert Brooks. Brooks dumps his girlfriend and then realizes he can't live without her. An attempt to say something about how single men feel about their situation. The answer, according to Brooks, who wrote and directed the film, is: miserable and depressed.

• *The Lonely Guy*, 1984, with Steve Martin. Another single man who can't hack it on his own. Seeing this and *Modern Romance* as a double feature is oppressive. If men are really this unhappy being single, why is it so hard to get them to the altar?

• *About Last Night*, 1986, with Rob Lowe and Demi Moore. A romance nurtured at a singles bar could be the real thing. A very sexy movie. Chemistry to burn between Lowe and Moore.

The Graduate, Part II: Love Will Tear Us Apart

It has been twenty years since anyone's heard from Benjamin or Elaine. When last seen, they were boarding a bus in Los Angeles. He was wearing sweats and tennis shoes. She was dressed in a long white bridal gown and veil. They were both out of breath from having just run away from her wedding.

For a long time after *The Graduate* came out, I used to argue with my friends about the meaning of this final scene. It was practically a Rorschach test on the need of people to believe—or disbelieve—that love could conquer all. The hopeless romantics in my crowd insisted Benjamin and Elaine lived happily ever after together, but that was not the way the rest of us saw it. To us, it was clear that the two already were beginning to realize they had made a terrible mistake aborting Elaine's wedding— which explains why they had nothing to say to each other on the bus. Elaine was thinking that her parents would never forgive her, and even Benjamin, who had no bridges left to burn, was concerned that he had sounded like a maniac screaming, "E-lainee," at the church.

My generation totally identified with these sorry lovers. I had a friend who, immediately after seeing the film, bought a red Alfa Romeo convertible like the one Benjamin drove across California in his mad dash to save Elaine from a marriage he was convinced was a mistake. We understood Benjamin's alienation because we, too, were a little worried about our future. We understood Elaine's confusion, especially the women among us who felt pushed too soon into married life. And, twenty years later, some of us even understand how Elaine's mother could have been attracted to Benjamin.

I wonder what became of Benjamin and Elaine the way I might wonder about old college chums. Since I've heard nothing about *The Graduate, Part II* being in the works—which is probably

219

just as well, since it could never equal the original—I thought I'd come up with my own scenario:

Benjamin was depressed for months after Elaine got off the bus without him. Her parting words were that she never wanted to see him again. This time, he believed her.

He went back to moping around his parents' house, until they finally threw him out. With no money and no other offers, he accepted a job with a family friend who was in the plastics business.

All the energy Benjamin had put into pursuing Elaine went into his work. He proved a genius at it. He came up with the idea of plastic containers for soda pop, shampoo and toothpaste. But his real claim to fame—the one that won him the title of Plastics King—was inventing the plastic grocery bag.

He became such a workaholic that his parents urged him to try doing nothing for a while. They secretly hoped he would meet a nice girl and settle down, but were afraid to say anything. They still felt guilty for having pushed him to get together with Elaine.

Elaine became a hippie after leaving Benjamin. She grew so weary of men, she joined a feminist collective. There, she blossomed into a real leader, organizing many of the major protests, including one against topless clubs. She never forgot the time Benjamin had forced her to watch a topless dancer.

Elaine realized that the skills she had developed in the movement could be applied to other things, like making money. She went back to college to study business and did so well that she got into a top MBA program, from which she graduated with honors.

A chain of grocery stores hired her. Elaine was on the corporate fast track, headed for a top management position.

As one of the team making the decision on whether the stores would use plastic grocery bags, she was asked to meet with the CEO of the plastics company. When he came into her office, she did a double take. "Benjamin," she said. "E-lainee," he said.

If He Can't Talk, He's Gonna Walk

"I believe in *this*," Ellen Barkin says, snapping her fingers in Al Pacino's face in *Sea of Love*. By *this*, she means animal attraction—that jarring feeling when you meet someone you instantly desire. Barkin's character doesn't waste any time acting on her desires. She goes to bed with men first and talks to them later. (Since her lovers have a habit of turning up dead, there's not much opportunity for real conversation.)

I haven't heard such a blanket endorsement of unpremeditated sex in years. It runs counter to the cautious way singles keep saying they behave. Does the screenwriter know something I don't?

The same day I saw *Sea of Love*, an article crossed my desk about the latest fad among New York singles: the talking date.

Men and women described first, second and even third dates in which they simply talked about their secret fears and dreams. They called these evenings "uncontrived meetings of the minds," and said they felt closer after one of them than if they had slept together.

I believe in *this*, but I'm also all for talking dates. There's an excitement in discovering how someone's mind works that can be every bit as thrilling as figuring out the rest of his or her anatomy. I could never be attracted to anyone I couldn't click with on an intellectual as well as physical level. Oh, I might get a twinge looking at a guy across a crowded room. But if his words didn't turn me on, the feeling would evaporate like dry ice.

The kind of attraction I believe in is, I suppose, more human than animal, since it is our ability to talk intelligently—as opposed to just making noise—that distinguishes us from other mammals. Without that, what do you really have? My idea of the "Date from Hell" would be to run out of things to say after hello. It wouldn't matter if I were out with Al Pacino; I'd still wish I

221

were in bed with a book.

Unlike other incompatibilities, there is no known treatment for verbal incompatibility. You just sit and stare at each other until you can't stand it anymore. I've seen couples in restaurants say nothing through four courses. They've looked awfully uncomfortable. It is hard to imagine them going home and making mad passionate love.

From the stories male friends have told me about their terrific sexual relations with bimbos, it may be that men don't absolutely require sparkling conversation before and after. My only experience with a bimbo equivalent was in high school, when I dated a football player. I'm not saying all football players are dumb, but mine sure was. He used "duh" as if it were an article. Despite how cute he looked in his uniform, I stopped seeing him after a few dates. There just wasn't any challenge.

However, animal attraction alone is enough to sustain men, or so they say. I think women crave more. I know I do. "You really need the talking component," an old boyfriend used to say. Often, he would say it when I was talking too much or during inappropriate moments when he wanted me to shut up.

Actually, I need the talking component and *this*—a combination that has been pretty hard to find. When I have stumbled upon it, it has made me a little crazy. I've thought I wouldn't survive another moment without seeing the object of my attraction or at least hearing his voice.

One nice thing about getting a little older is that you can have these romantic thoughts and laugh at them at the same time. That's called perspective. It's never simple to be swept away by whatever you want to call it—passion, lust, love, *this*. However, in these times it is more complicated than ever. Do you go for it like the woman in *Sea of Love* or do you sit down and talk about it? Whatever you decide, be grateful for the feeling. Some people only experience it vicariously at the movies.

A Movie's Dissonant Ring of Truth

Fatal Attraction starts out as a chilling study of a woman who loves too much. Her self-destructive behavior when she gets involved with a married man is sure to bring gasps of recognition from women in the audience. But nobody could identify with her by the last scene. She becomes a knife-wielding wacko, possessed not by love but by the spirit of Norman Bates.

I wish the filmmakers had resisted the urge to turn *Fatal Attraction* into *Psycho IV*, because they really were onto something: Theirs is the most accurate portrayal I've seen of this type of obsession. I know women who have done every single thing that Alex Forest does in the movie except pick up a knife. I've done one or two of them myself.

From appearances—a good job as a book editor in New York, great looks, a fabulous apartment she put together herself—Alex seems to have too much going for her to be so unhappy over a man. That's what I keep telling my friends, too.

It's a classic syndrome, and the movie takes us through it step by step:

• *Fall for the wrong man.* "Why is it that all the interesting guys are always married?" Alex asks Dan after spending a passionate night with him when his wife is away. They're not; it's just that those are the men women like Alex are attracted to. They seem to seek out relationships that are doomed from the beginning.
• *Don't take no for an answer.* Dan wants out after the first night, but there is no way he can get Alex to accept this. She is relentless about pursuing him: repeatedly calling his office, showing up there uninvited, phoning him at home and hanging up when his wife answers. Surely those phone calls will ring a bell.
• *Make yourself as miserable as possible.* Alex buys a pair of opera tickets, hoping that Dan will go with her. The ticket ploy is a

familiar one. How can he say no after you've gone to all that trouble and expense? But Dan does say no. In what was to my mind the movie's most frightening scene, Alex holes up in her darkened apartment and stares at the tickets, illuminated by a light she flicks on and off.

• *Build a fleeting affair into your main reason for living.* All of Alex's energy is consumed by Dan. I kept wondering how she managed to get any work done. Romances like this take on a life of their own. Because they're so one-sided, one person—and it could just as well be the man—has to do all the work.

Besides obsessional love, *Fatal Attraction* touches on the fear single women over thirty-five have that they will never give birth. It can't be accidental that Alex is thirty-six. When Alex tells Dan she is pregnant with his child, he is surprised she had not used birth control. Never mind that he didn't, either, and never thought to discuss the issue with her. Like most men, he is hardly blameless. But that's another story.

Alex says she had a bad miscarriage and didn't think she could get pregnant. She seems thrilled about this development. It may be her last chance to have a baby, she says. In a case of life-imitating-film, I got a call a few days after seeing *Fatal Attraction* from a thirty-six-year-old friend who is pregnant under almost identical circumstances.

Because so much in *Fatal Attraction* is true to life, it had the chance to really hit people where they love. I read that it originally had a much less violent ending, but it was changed, based on comments from preview audiences. I don't doubt that a lot of people go to movies these days to see blood. But they could have gotten something quite different out of this film. They could have seen light.

A Modern Question
of Morals

Jane Craig, the heroine of *Broadcast News*, is very much a twenti-eth-century woman. She has a profession, not just a job, as a TV news producer, and she is damn good at it. She is smart and sassy, and if that puts off men, well, that's their problem.

One man who seems intrigued by her attitude is Tom Grunick, a good-looking but none-too-bright correspondent at the network where she works. Jane acts more like the heroine of a nineteenth-century novel when she rejects this suitor based solely on his character. All is going well between them until she discovers that, to further his career, Tom has done something she considers immoral.

That puts an end to their budding romance. She can overlook his mind, especially while looking into his eyes, but not his values. Like a novel by Jane Austen or the Brontë sisters, the movie seems to be saying that a man's moral fiber matters more than anything else about him.

Such a quaint notion is hardly ever heard anymore. It is hard enough in these tenuous times to find someone you care about without making trouble for yourself by wondering whether he or she is morally fit. During all the talks I've had with girlfriends about a particular man, we have discussed his sense of humor, his love-making technique, his teeth, his salary, but never, as I recall, his character. The closest we came was to dismiss him as a jerk. However, that just meant he was being a jerk by not calling or by going out with another woman. His jerkiness wasn't held against him if he changed his mind and became interested again.

Looking back on the men in my life, I can now see which of them had character and which were just characters. I once went out with a guy who bossed around anyone he considered below him—which included most people. He acted as if he were a feudal landlord. Although I knew that was wrong, I didn't stop

225

going out with him until I, too, got the serf treatment.

What is so noble about Jane's action is that it is not based on the way Tom behaves toward her. He seeks her out. He respects her. He may even love her. Certainly, he wouldn't do anything to hurt her. But deep down he is not the kind of person she can respect and, to her, that is a fatal flaw.

Broadcast News is a very smart movie, and it may have spotted a trend. Perhaps character—which already has made a comeback in politics—will do the same in relationships. The film got me thinking about what qualities count in another person, how to discern them and what difference, if any, it makes.

Suppose you met someone who seemed wonderful and this someone began to pay a lot of attention to you. Would it matter if you found out that he or she had padded an expense account? Or robbed a bank? I can't answer that for you. I can't even answer it for myself. But I do know that it's easier to take a moral stand and dump the cheat or robber if you are not head over heels in love with him.

Every person has his or her own set of moral beliefs. It is hard to see much future in a relationship where two people's belief systems are diametrically opposed. The tricky part is to find that out before your feelings get involved.

Jane waited too long. By the time she discovered the flaw in Tom's character, she already was thinking this might be it. But she had something she believed in more than the two of them: her profession.

I'm not sure I would have been strong enough to have made the choice she did—especially with someone who looks like William Hurt waiting for me at the airport. But I can see that she did the right thing. A person's character may not seem to matter in the throes of a romance. But, in the long run, character does matter, as heroines have been discovering for centuries.

Sex, Women and Reality: The Sequel

I am confused by the sex part of *Sex, Lies and Videotape.*

Here is a movie about the sexual eccentricities of people in their twenties written and directed by a twenty-six-year-old who should know how to portray his own generation. Yet his two women characters seem to belong not to the present but to the past—specifically to my past.

Ann reminds me of the nice girls I grew up with who kept their sexuality in check because that was what you did in the early '60s. They married young, which was also what you did then, and found they couldn't simply turn on the desire they had dutifully turned off.

By contrast, Cynthia, with her tousled hair and thigh-high skirts, is like the bad girls whose sexual exploits were whispered about and secretly envied by us nice girls. The soap-opera twist is that the two are sisters, and Cynthia is sleeping with Ann's husband—which is more than Ann is doing. "I'm kinda goin' through this thing where I don't want him to touch me," she tells her shrink.

An old college chum of her husband's comes to visit. This fellow has an eccentricity of his own: videotaping women's most intimate sexual secrets. He gets Ann to confess she thinks sex is overrated. (How many times did I used to hear that from female friends who were afraid or unable to let go in bed?) Ann sublimates her sexual feelings the same way those women did—by passionately cleaning her house. (She is home a lot because her husband has told her he doesn't want her to work. Do men still say things like that? Do women listen?)

Meanwhile, her sister's skimpy outfits get progressively more bizarre. Instead of looking sexually liberated, Cynthia looks deranged, which is what we used to fear too much sex would do to you.

227

I hadn't realized until watching *Sex, Lies and Videotape* that the nice girl/bad girl dichotomy still exists. I assumed women in their twenties had grown up with the message that sex was not only O.K. but great fun, and they could be nice and bad simultaneously.

Wasn't that what the sexual revolution was all about? It started quietly with books and classes for "pre-orgasmic" women. (I always thought that was a more hopeful way of putting it than calling them nonorgasmic. At some point during the '70s, my generation of women got real aggressive about our right to be sexual. We would brag about our conquests; we sounded like men.

I recall a friend who was having a hot affair with a married man around this time saying contemptuously, "His wife doesn't even enjoy sex." That seemed to be at once an ample excuse for continuing the affair and the worse thing that could be said of another woman.

We scared away numerous would-be lovers before we finally calmed down. Our little revolution ended not with a bang but a whimper—actually more like a sigh of relief that sex didn't have to be a battle anymore. I took it for granted that because we went through all this craziness, younger women wouldn't have to. Now along comes a time-warp movie to make me question my assumption.

A male friend, whose sexual experience spans the generations, tells me I am naive to believe women in their twenties have sex figured out. He says that if anything they have a harder time coping with hang-ups, precisely because all their lives they've been told they should enjoy sex, whereas women my age had no such expectation.

Maybe so, but *Sex, Lies and Videotape* still seems dated to me.

For instance, if women today were to sublimate their desires (as well they may, if for no other reason than lack of available men), it would be with massages, facials, pedicures or the other hands-on treatments that have become so popular—not with housework.

I have a sixth sense about being able to tell whether a woman is into sex. There is an ease about the way she moves. Skimpy attire has nothing to do with it.

I certainly hope women no longer believe they have to be either like Ann or like Cynthia. There's no real evidence that they do. After all, *Sex, Lies and Videotape* is only a movie. Or is it?

Face It: A Man's Job Does Matter

As we were leaving the theater after seeing *Crossing Delancey*, my friend Mark wanted to know whether there really are old-world marriage brokers like the one in the movie. This woman claimed to be able to find anyone a nice Jewish mate, provided you weren't too particular. Her motto was: "Ya look, ya meet, ya try, ya see."

I was surprised at Mark's interest in marriage brokers. He hardly needs help meeting women. Just the other day, he met someone while double-parked in front of a grocery store. But the movie had gotten him thinking that maybe it was time to find a nice Jewish girl from a good family and settle down, and for that he didn't know where to look.

I suspect *Crossing Delancey* may affect a lot of single people this way. All of us independent types are sure to identify with Izzy, the film's heroine, who turns her back on her ethnic heritage to establish her own identity. She insists she is happy living alone in a tiny apartment in uptown New York and working at a fashionable bookstore. Her grandmother, however, can't understand how Izzy could have reached thirty and still not have a husband.

To remedy that, "Bubbie" (the Yiddish word for grandmother) consults a marriage broker. The latter finds for Izzy—whose literary pretensions have led her into the arms of famous writers for whom she is a mere dalliance—a sincere, if plodding, pickle merchant. Against all odds, Izzy falls for him.

You don't have to be Jewish to get the movie's message:

229

Listen to your elders and get married already and be sure it's to one of your own kind.

It happens that *Crossing Delancey* came out around the Jewish High Holidays, when Jews feel the strongest pull toward family and tradition. Those who are single were especially receptive to the movie's message. After hearing it delivered by Izzy's Bubbie, I called my aunt in Miami Beach to wish her a happy holiday. (Because my mother and both grandmothers are gone, she plays the role of Bubbie in my life.)

"Happy New Year," I said. There was a long silence. Finally, my aunt spoke.

"Oh," she said, "I thought you were calling to tell me you're getting married."

My aunt has never made a big deal about my marrying within the faith. She has often said it is more important that my intended be a good person. However, if he is going to be a louse—except she didn't say louse, she said, "shtunk," the Yiddish equivalent—then better he be a Jewish shtunk.

She should be assured that I go out only with nice men. However, I have to admit that what they do for a living is more important to me than their religion, which is the basic quarrel I have with *Crossing Delancey*. The film seems to say that as long as a guy is Jewish and nice, it shouldn't matter if he is a butcher, a baker or a pickle maker. But if Izzy is anything like me or the other career women I know, a man's occupation does matter.

I do not seek out men because they make a lot of money. But I like to go out with someone I can talk to about his work. Since I talk constantly about mine, our conversations would be pretty one-sided otherwise. Somehow I just don't think that anyone who makes pickles would want to discuss them in his spare time. And, at the risk of sounding like a snob, I have to admit that if he did, I wouldn't want to hear about it.

Izzy's pickle merchant tells her that work doesn't define him. Yet a woman who has had to support herself as many years as Izzy has will have found that her job consumes a great deal of her life—probably more of it than religion.

I am talking about what is important in another person with whom you might conceivably settle down. The marriage broker has her theory; I have mine.

Women and Men Really Can Be Pals

I give thumbs-up to the movie *Roxanne*, and not just for the imaginative way it turns the story of *Cyrano de Bergerac* on its nose. More than the unlikely romance between Steve Martin, as the guy with the big schnoz, and Daryl Hannah, I was taken by the best-buddy relationship he carries on with Shelley Duvall. As unbelievable as the film is at times, that relationship rings absolutely true. It captures the essence of a friendship between a man and a woman: the lack of any competition or jealousy.

Martin confides his feelings about Hannah to Duvall, babbling on to an extent that would be humiliating had he been talking to a man. And by figuring out how to get Hannah to see there is more to Martin than his nose, Duvall instinctively puts his happiness before her own. If the thought occurred to her that by turning him over to another woman, she might lose him herself, it certainly doesn't inhibit her.

I wish there had been more scenes between Martin and Duvall, but it's not hard to figure out why there weren't. Let's face it: Platonic relationships, by definition, aren't sexy—whether acted out on screen or off.

I get a little tired of hearing them denigrated as a result. Why do people deny romantic involvements by saying, "We're just friends"—as if that status were easier to attain than one of lover? And, when an affair breaks up, why are the parting words inevitably, "Can't we just be friends?"—as if that were a consolation prize? As one who has several male pals, let me tell you there is nothing second-rate about these relationships. What we have together is in a sense better than marriage, because we *aren't* bound to each other in the way that makes couples fantasize

231

about divorce, if not murder.

Boyfriends and even a husband have come and gone, but my men friends are still here. I have found our association goes on after the men marry, which hasn't always been true with women friends. It may be that because women have a better understanding of friendship, they can handle their husbands continuing to see an old buddy, even a female one.

At its most basic level, a friendship is a friendship. Still, there is something special about ones between the opposite sex. My male friends and I go to parties together, knowing there will be no hurt feelings if I meet someone and leave with him. I turn to them for a man's perspective on why the fellow I was dating stopped calling. And during those dateless stretches, I appreciate the attention from my men friends all the more. However, for this kind of relationship to work, you must be like brother and sister. If there are any sexual feelings—especially if just one person feels them—the friendship is in trouble.

Some people have a hard time understanding how a man and a woman could hang out together without being sexually attached. That's how rumors get started. When I've been out on the town with Hans, a European gentleman of a certain age, we have caught people staring at us, obviously trying to figure out the nature of our relationship. Hans has jokingly suggested I introduce him as my Sugar Daddy. But he is something much better. He's my friend.

A SINGULAR PERSPECTIVE

The time has come to begin to enjoy your life. To do so starts with acceptance, which is different from resignation. Accept that you may be single for a long time, possibly forever, and begin to believe you can have a swell time anyway. Remember the Pollyanna advice to count your blessings? Well, start counting. You've got your health, a good job, good friends and a family who care about you and probably worry about you, too. So why shouldn't you be happy?

You should look to successful singles as role models instead of to married people. The opportunities are there for singles to lead productive lives in the '90s. Women have never had it so good in terms of the careers open to them.

You'll know you have made a singular adjustment to the single life when you stop looking to role models at all and look to yourself.

Welcome to the Decade of Singles!

The '70s were known as the "Me" decade, the '80s as the "Greed" decade. Though the '90s have only just begun, already there's a move to come up with a catchy name for them. How about the "Just Me" decade, in recognition of single people finally coming into our own? Instead of being the nobodies we've been for the past ninety years, we seem poised to have a major impact on mores in the last gasp of the century.

It's traditional for the new year to offer some predictions and resolutions, and I'm going to give you both. Those who pore over census figures predict that at some point during the '90s, half the population of the United States will be single, including the divorced and the widowed, along with perennial bachelors and bachelorettes. Based on that, I predict:

• The people who run businesses and run for office are about to figure out that singles are consumers and voters, too.
• By the 1996 election, if not sooner, it will be politically incorrect for presidential candidates to talk—as they did in 1988—about the needs of the nuclear family without giving a nod to the desires of singles.
• Housing experts, trying to figure out how to build a family home that a family can actually afford, also will consider economical ways to house single dwellers.
• There will be equal room on grocery shelves for super-economy size and single-serving products.
• Maîtres d' will be delighted to seat parties of one instead of grimacing and insisting that all the empty tables have been reserved for two or more—whether or not that happens to be true.

As gratifying as affirmation from the outside will be, it won't sustain us unless we, too, come to terms with our single status. People have to stop seeing it as second-class citizenship or a phase we are going through. We should accept the possibility, though not the inevitability, that it could be permanent and get on with our lives.

Here are the rest of my resolutions for my fellow singles. Resolve to:

• *Keep yourself entertained.* Start with simple things, such as going for long walks or bike rides or reading the Sunday paper in a café instead of cooped up in your apartment. Put some time into planning your social life; don't just expect it to happen. Check the entertainment listings and buy tickets to the events that interest you so you are committed to going. Plan to have people over. Don't just think about it. Actually invite them. Join a gym, go to a lecture, get involved in some kind of organization—singles, religious, group therapy—in which people sit around talking.

• *Take advantage of being single.* Think of all the spontaneous things you can do that your married friends can't, at least not without consulting each other. You can stay up as late as you want reading or eat whenever you're hungry or hop in your car and get out of town. If you've got the bucks, you can also take a trip at the spur of the moment wherever you want to go.

• *Be more independent.* Learn to rely on your own instincts about purchasing a car or making investments, or deciding whether the new person in your life is worth your time. Stop making decisions by polling all your friends on what they think.

• *Be more aggressive about meeting people.* Talk to strangers (as long as others are around, so you're not taking a real risk). Start conversations in groceries or restaurants or on the bus. The problem many singles have meeting people is that they don't seem to grasp that the people they see every day are potential dates.

• *Do not make yourself unhappy.* Singles are experts at this. We can drive ourselves crazy with thoughts of how our lives are not turning out the way they were supposed to and how we'll never find anyone to love. The danger of thinking these thoughts is that they can become self-fulfilling prophecies.

• *Stop seeing marriage as some kind of panacea.* If you hate your job or your nose when you're single, I can promise you'll still hate them after you've said, "I do." Don't settle for just anyone because he or she is better than no one. The worst hell is to go through life with someone you don't really love.

• *Have a happy new decade!* The '90s are yours. Make the most of them.

Role Models for Singles Hard to Find

I feel a pang every time I pick up a story I think is going to be about Diane Sawyer's TV show and find myself reading how divinely happy she is since she got married.

Her relationship with Sam Donaldson I can handle. But I would just as soon not know that she and Mike Nichols embrace in the street and that she blurts out, "Oh, my wonderful husband!" when he shows up unexpectedly to take her home from work. I'm not jealous so much as resentful. While Mike was gaining a partner in wonderfulness, I was losing a role model.

Diane was the kind of single I aspire to be. She always seemed so confident on her own. I imagined she could handle anything— from a mouse in the kitchen to a louse in the bedroom. Her salary from the networks guaranteed her financial independence. I wouldn't go so far as to call money a prerequisite for a successful single life, but it sure helps. Looking at her, you just knew she was single by choice, not because she hadn't had any proposals. (One of the more bizarre offers came from Sylvester Stallone's mother, who let it be known via a gossip columnist that she wanted her Sly to marry Diane.)

I actually approve of the man to whom she finally said yes. I feel a little silly admitting this, but *I* would marry Mike Nichols—

and I've never even met him. Still, for my own selfish reason, I wish she had held out. It's not going to be easy to find another role model who gives being single the same cachet Diane did.

To qualify, a woman must be famous, interesting and of a certain age, so that her singleness is not merely a stage she is going through. (The age I have in mind is about as old as I am.) She should have a life I should be so lucky to be leading. It also helps if she has been profiled in *Vanity Fair*, which is how I learn where she stands on the Big Questions, such as Would she ever get married? and Why hasn't she?

Another Diane—Diane Keaton—comes close to meeting my criteria. She talks an independent talk, and she has got to be interesting to have attracted Woody Allen, Warren Beatty and Al Pacino. However, while Diane S. seemed sure about everything she did, including remaining single, Diane K. strikes me as a doubter. It may be her indelible Annie Hall image, rather than the way she really is, that makes me envision her on the phone moaning to a girlfriend.

"I don't know, maybe I should have married Woody," I imagine her saying, twirling her hair and dissolving into what a shrink would call inappropriate laughter. "I mean, now it looks like I won't ever marry. Um, do you think I'll be O.K.?"

I certainly envy Jacqueline Bisset's astonishing looks for a woman of the aforementioned age and the exotic traveling she does for her movie roles. But *Vanity Fair* describes her as a homebody who would just as soon stay put in her "cozy French country house" in Southern California—which isn't my style. And she has been in and out of several long-term relationships that sound too much like marriages for my taste. "I don't feel self-sufficient, no," she told VF.

That leaves another Jacqueline: Jackie Onassis. I realize she is older than the rest of us, but, hey, I'm not going to be ageist about this role-model business. I admire Jackie O. for going out and getting a job, especially since she doesn't have to work. But her attitude toward men knocks her out of the running. According to *Vanity Fair*, Jackie—who complained that JFK wouldn't help her decide what dress to wear—defers all the time to her current beau, Maurice Tempelsman. At dinner parties at her home, she will turn to him and ask, "Maurice, should we have coffee here or in the living room?"

Can you imagine Diane Sawyer ever asking Mike that? I may have to face the fact that there will never be another Diane. Maybe I should stop searching for a role model—and start looking up to myself.

A New Baby Boom, Old Questions

I thought, I have played this game before. We had been instructed to name twenty-six items—one starting with each letter of the alphabet—that the guest of honor, who was eight months pregnant, would soon be carting around. The mothers in the group started scribbling away. The rest of us looked stumped. I left "A" blank and, under "B," wrote "baby," though I knew that couldn't be right.

I have played this game before. It was twenty years ago, during my first round of baby showers. I knew even less about motherhood then, but I fully expected to learn. The mother-to-be, as well as the other guests at those showers, would have been twenty something. Watching her tearing off the baby-blue and pink wrapping paper and exclaiming over the tiny offerings, I imagined one day that would be me.

Now when I go to a baby shower, everybody there, including mama-to-be, is forty something. I am like the perennial bridesmaid; I no longer expect to someday be the center of attention; I no longer expect to be expecting. I don't mean to sound maudlin. I have more or less come to terms with not having children. People can't have everything they want. (That's actually a line from Edward Albee, but I have said it to myself so many times during my inner monologues about children that I feel as if it's mine.)

When I was nearing forty, I decided I had to let go of the baby fantasy. My life was clearly heading in another direction. I could either go with it or drive myself nuts thinking about what I was missing. I went with it. I hadn't figured on more baby showers.

I hadn't figured so many women my age would decide to have children, even if it meant undergoing mortifying treatments for infertility or, if all else failed, adopting. Or that single friends would deliberately get pregnant because it was now or never. Most of all, I hadn't figured on the effect their decisions would have on me.

Every time I hear another friend is going to be a mother, I wonder whether I should be doing the same. Will my life really be O.K. without children? Or will I regret not having them when I'm old? Having spent my adult life trying not to get pregnant, I am suddenly obsessed with a need to know whether I even can.

In any other era, a forty-five-year-old single woman surely would not question whether she should remain childless. It would seem as if there were no other choice. As much as anything, my confusion is a result of all the options now available to women. The only way I know to shut off my inner monologue is to distance myself from babies and baby talk. I go to friends' showers. (How could I not, knowing how much the occasion means to them?) However, I sit far away from the present-opening and the games, and I leave early.

An old friend called the other day from the East Coast to ask whether she and her year-old son could stay with me for a week. I thought about my white couch and cream carpets and the porcelain statues perched precariously on my fireplace mantel. I thought about my peace and quiet being shattered along with the statues. I envisioned all the paraphernalia mothers bring with them strewn around my apartment. (I may not be able to name the items, but I know there are a lot of them.) I told her this wasn't a good time.

These are perfectly legitimate reasons to say no. But I wonder whether there wasn't yet another reason. This friend is one of the women I mentioned who decided not to wait for a husband to

241

have a baby. She has always been more willing to take risks than I have, leaving a good job in San Francisco for an unknown future as a free-lance photographer. The baby was her biggest risk, but, as with everything else in her life, it has turned out fine. The imagined problems that have stopped me from seriously considering single motherhood have not materialized for her. Susan is managing on her own. She adores being a mother. She is the happiest she has ever been.

I want her to be happy. I want all my friends who recently have become mothers to be happy. I'm just not sure I'm prepared to see close up how happy they are.

Thoughts That Haunt Singles' Lonely Hours

You're more likely to be happy if you get married than if you remain single. That has been a consistent finding of almost every survey conducted on the subject, though a recent study at least shows the happiness gap between marrieds and unmarrieds to have narrowed.

You might think single people would be *happier* than married ones. If other people have the capacity to make us happy, they can also make up supremely unhappy. Look through a divorce lawyer's files sometime if you don't believe me. Where singles have the edge, however, is that we can make ourselves miserable without anyone's help. I know of no other group quite so adept at it.

Just thinking about how happy everybody who is married must be is enough to get you started. You could drive yourself crazy imagining happy families conversing happily around the dining room table while you sit glumly alone at the kitchen counter. Singles have other distressing thoughts but might not talk about them outside of a therapist's office. I'm going to enumerate a few, so you'll know you're not alone in thinking them, should that make you any happier—or unhappier, if you prefer:

• *Your life is not turning out the way it was supposed to.* On some level, every single person thinks he or she really should be married. No matter how successful or—heaven forbid—happy you may be, if you've reached a certain age and are still single, you're stuck with this nagging feeling you've done something wrong.

• *Nobody loves you.* The proof is that nobody calls you. Single people need a lot of assurance of friendship, more than married couples who have each other. That's why phone-answering machines shouldn't be allowed in the homes of singles. You start measuring your worth by the number of calls you have received. On those days—and we all have them—when there are no messages, you assume that means nobody cares about you.

• *You need a baby to make you happy.* This thought usually pops into your mind around Father's or Mother's Day. Suddenly, you start seeing adorable kids everywhere and envying their parents. It gets to the point where you can't bear to look at one more darling daughter riding on her father's shoulders or another pregnant woman radiating happiness.

• *You'll never find someone to love.* The infamous Harvard–Yale study on the sorry odds of getting married confirmed the worst fear of single people: There really isn't anybody out there. The subsequent reports saying your chances aren't as bad as all that didn't help any. Why look on the bright side when you can take a dim view?

• *You can do better than the person you did find.* This is a sure-fire way to make yourself unhappy even if you are lucky enough to be in a relationship with someone who really cares about you. Decide he or she isn't good enough for you. You can then torment yourself with all the people you could be dating.

There are some easy remedies to stop being unhappy in these particular ways. You could throw out your phone machine. Or find people whose children have become juvenile delinquents and ask them how wonderful it is to be a parent. Or check out

243

some of the losers other people have actually married. None of these, however, gets at the heart of what is really troubling single people. I'm not sure I know exactly what it is, beyond the pressure we feel to conform to whatever we grew up thinking we should be doing with our lives, and the simple fact that it is harder to go it alone.

But this I do know: Just as you can choose to be unhappy, you can choose to be happy. I remember Ruth Gordon, one of the happiest people I ever interviewed, saying, "Stuff gets in the way, sweep it under the rug." Why don't we do that with all these unhappy thoughts? The next time a sociologist calls to ask whether you're happy, say, "Yes."

Don't Pity Me 'Cause I Want to Be Alone

Bit by bit, I am turning into a loner. The transformation appears to be out of my control, in the same way that Jeff Goldblum couldn't keep from sprouting wings in *The Fly*. I am aware of the change in me, although I can only speculate why it might be happening. I wonder if it has to do with living alone (has the Surgeon General ever studied the long-term effects of that?), or whether I'm going through your basic midlife crisis—which could happen to anyone, even a married person.

At any rate, I have been seduced by solitude. I never knew it could be so—well—calming.

I prefer to be alone among other people rather than shut up in my house. I seek out cafés, movie theaters, aerobics classes—the kind of places where one can be an anonymous face or body in the crowd, yet still get a sense of life going on, without which I fear I might really become weird. I used to at least try to find a companion to do things with—not because I was afraid to do them alone, but because it seemed more sociable. Now I no longer make the effort. I would just as soon go by myself. I have little interest anymore in the chitchat that nourishes friendships, particularly between women. I talk to myself instead. (No, not out loud, although, like most loners, I'm afraid it will come to that.)

The most revolutionary change is that I've stopped discussing my love life with girlfriends. I don't feel the need to report every date as if it were a late-breaking news story. (Would men be flattered or appalled if they realized how much time women spend talking about them? Just wondering.)

I remember the first romance I clammed up about. It was going so well I was afraid I might jinx it. Besides, the man was one of those private types. I was quite sure he would be appalled to find himself Topic A. Anyway, those were the reasons I gave for my silence. But a good friend, who had listened to me talking endlessly about other men, accused me of "withdrawing." In retrospect, she may have been more right than I was. As I have continued to withdraw, it has made me question whether one can be a loner and also have close friends.

I've understood since grade school the importance of sharing confidences. Girls trade secrets the way boys trade baseball cards. If you have nothing to trade, nobody is going to tell you anything. When you grow up and have an answering machine, if you never make the first call, eventually nobody is going to leave a message. You can't go back and forth from loner to Miss Congeniality. For instance, I still get an occasional urge to chat, maybe even about men. However, my friends, who went through a period of being hurt by my lack of attention—"You don't call, you don't write," they would say, only half joking—have become accustomed to it.

Now when I do call, they assume I have an urgent reason. There's an awkward pause after they've said hello and I've said hello, when they're obviously waiting for me to get to the point. How can I tell them I just want to talk?

Being a loner isn't for sissies. It fortifies me to know I am in good company. Jackie Onassis, Gene Hackman, Katharine Hepburn, Giants slugger Will Clark and, of course, Garbo all revealed themselves to be loners. "I don't need anybody," Will the Thrill personally told me. "I'm happy going to a movie by myself. I sit in the middle of the theater in the dark and nobody knows who I am." (I'd rather you thought we wound up alone together at the same movie theater, but actually he said it to me in an interview, not in the dark.)

Because they share a common root, the assumption could be made that loners are by definition lonely. However, I make a distinction between people such as Will and I, who are loners by choice, and those who really don't have any friends. I am not—repeat, *not*—lonely. Sometimes I worry about doing too well alone and how that affects my prospects of ever marrying again. Basically, I like keeping myself entertained. I like keeping my own counsel. I like keeping secrets.

A Nagging Fear of Old Age

The first time I saw her in the neighborhood—a well-dressed, silver-haired woman of a certain age pushing a luggage cart piled high with suitcases—I thought of offering to help. But I was afraid that might sound condescending, and, anyway, she seemed to be managing fine.

I was puzzled when I noticed her a few days later wandering up and down the street with the same cart full of suitcases. Had she gone somewhere and come back? And, if so, where was she off to this time? Having seen her dozens more times, it's become apparent that the poor woman isn't going anywhere, except around in circles. I've come to think of her as an upscale bag lady, hoarding her belongings in suitcases instead of shopping bags.

I know nothing about this woman. It could be that she has six children whom she has so alienated that they don't care what she does and a husband who helps her pack every morning just to get her out of the house. However, I imagine a very different life for her. In the fantasy I have concocted, she is single and lives alone, possibly with a cat or cats. She has no family nearby to look after her and no close friends. In other words, I've made her into somebody who could be me in twenty-five years.

My neighborhood luggage lady plays into one of the worst fears of single people: the fear that spending so much time by yourself will make you weird (assuming you don't start out that way).

We may be basically content with our lives for now, but we're a little worried about our future. We've established that it's O.K. to be single when you're young and everybody else is in the same boat, and we're finding that we can handle it in middle age. But, whether or not we admit it, we're terrified of growing old on our own.

It should be reassuring to learn that studies on aging have shown that singles handle old age better than any other group. That doesn't surprise me. We are, by and large, a resourceful lot, used to taking care of ourselves and doing things alone—skills that are hard to develop in later life. Singles do not experience the pain and loneliness that married people do when they lose a spouse or when their children move away and forget to call or write.

I once lived in an apartment building with a lot of elderly widows. They would congregate in the lobby waiting for the postman. They looked so disappointed when he had no letters for them. When you're single, you don't depend on mail for your happiness.

Singles often have an extensive network of friends. Friends play an important role as you grow older. Because they are close to you out of choice—not obligation—they can be more of a comfort during times of illness than members of your own family.

I know all these things to be true without having to read them. And yet the nagging feeling persists that there is something unnatural about growing old alone. I still have this Norman Rockwell picture in my head of a grandmother surrounded by family in her old age. But with no children, grandchildren are going to be hard to come by. I can be haughty now about not needing a husband. But it might be nice to have one around when independence is no longer such an intoxicant and when I might literally need someone to lean on.

It's a little scary to think about what kind of an old lady I will become. If I continue to be so set in my ways, by the time I reach sixty-five, I should be petrified. I can see myself lining up my Geritol bottles in a straight row and arranging my support-hose by color. I already talk to myself; by then, I should be answering back. It's hard to imagine not having the energy to do everything I do now. It's unthinkable that I might not have all my marbles.

Surely, in twenty-five years, I'll be packing for a trip around the world by myself. Or will I just be packing?

Slow the Rush to the Altar

I am staring at the results of a national survey conducted by Great Expectations, the country's largest video dating service, and I can't quite believe what I'm seeing. Fifty-six percent of single men and 72 percent of single women say they would like to get married within a year. Almost half the women are in such a rush that they talk about marriage and kids on a first date. And then they wonder why the guys don't call for a second date.

The personal ads are no longer filled with people looking for a good time; now they're looking for a spouse. Why is everybody suddenly so hot to get married? It's as if one of those slick ad agencies that convinced us to buy light beer and diet pop had done a subliminal campaign for marriage. Fear of AIDS and the diminishing chances of women marrying past age thirty-five are the apparent reasons for this frenzy to find a mate.

While I agree it's certainly better to be wed than dead, marriage is not the panacea it is being made out to be. I think people who have never been married have a naive notion of what it is all about. The more desirable the concept of marriage becomes, the higher their expectations—and the more likely they are to be disappointed. Marriage, it has been said, it like a besieged fortress. Everyone inside wants to get out and everyone outside wants to get in. Unfortunately, today too many people seem desperate to get in—to the point that they think it is better to be married to anyone than to be alone. It seems just yesterday that singles were bemoaning the pressure put on them to get married. Now they're putting the pressure on themselves.

Look, I don't know why you're not married. I'm not even sure I fully understand why I'm not. But you can't just wish things to be different. You'll only end up wishing your life away instead of enjoying the incredible freedom that comes with being single.

While everyone else hums a tune that sounds like "Goin' to the Chapel," I would like to sing the praises of the single life. I love not having to tell anyone how my day went. I love the solitude of my home late at night and early in the morning. I love going to sleep whenever I want. I love eating at 6:30 one evening and at midnight the next. I love not having to keep food in the house. I love planning dinner parties and inviting only the people I like—not my husband's friends. I love waking up on Saturday morning and knowing I can do anything I want with my week-end. I love going grocery shopping in the middle of the night and not having to explain where I have been.

I can't be the only single person with these feelings, or maybe it's just that having been married, I'm in a better position to appreciate going it alone.

Sociologist Darlaine Gardetto thinks the reason singles complain so much is that secretly they feel guilty about being able to do anything they want. "It's like eating a big box of chocolates lying in bed," she says. "You feel slovenly that you would be living such a life."

Sure, there are times when I wonder about the road not taken. I see families in the park and imagine what it would be like to be the mommy. But I also realize that if I had a husband and children, I couldn't go out every night or plan trips on the spur of the moment or not talk to anyone all day. All I am saying is that while there are many roads to happiness, the one sure route to unhappiness is to want desperately what you don't have.

The Twenties Aren't the Right Time to Get Married

Every time I talk to my twenty-one-year-old niece, I'm afraid she is going to tell me she's engaged. Don't get me wrong. I have nothing against her young man. I just don't want her to marry him. If John F. Kennedy, Jr., were to propose, I wouldn't want her to marry him, either. I'd like to see her be on her own for a while—a long while, say, until she's at least thirty. After she has had a chance to figure out who she is, she can marry anyone she wants, with my blessing.

I am trying to save her from making the mistake I made, which was marrying much too young. However, it's unlikely anything I say will have much effect. My niece is just as sure she knows what she is doing as I was at her age. I only hope she is not also just as wrong.

If a fairy godmother were to grant me one wish, I would ask for my twenties back. I want to spend them single. I want to bum around Europe with a knapsack and stay at youth hostels and have adventures. I want to fall in love dozens of times. I want to be a Cosmo girl.

My longing for the road not taken has little to do with the fact that the one I took led straight to divorce court. If my marriage had lasted, I believe I would still regret spending my twenties cocooning (before it was fashionable) instead of carousing. Actually, I might have regretted it more, since I did finally have some solo adventures, though not with the carefree abandon with which I imagine I would have had them if I had been younger.

I try to remember what my big rush was to get married. Part of it, I suppose, was a desire to grow up fast; being Mrs. Some-body sounded awfully grown-up. And part of it was fear. Some-one had always been there to take care of me, and I don't think it occurred to me I could take care of myself. The thought of living alone would have terrified me. Not that I ever thought of it—it was as inconceivable as living in a foreign country, another thing I wish I had done in my twenties.

But mine was a selective kind of timidity. I was timid in my personal life, but brazen as could be when it came to my profession. Fresh out of journalism school, I went down to the South Side of Chicago and talked myself into a job as the only white person and only woman at Jet magazine.

(Many mornings when I arrived at the office, I'd find a man occupying my desk who didn't work there, but seemed to know all the employees. He was organizing a self-help group for blacks on such a shoestring budget that office equipment was out of the question. He must have figured that, being the junior member of the staff, I didn't dare ask him to leave. He was right. And that's how I came to claim Jesse Jackson used my typewriter.)

I was like two different people during those years: the gutsy reporter covering race riots, and the good wife who was so afraid of saying the wrong thing that her in-laws thought she was shy. I never did find the real me within my marriage. That only happened after a wrenching divorce and a lot of living on my own.

I know people who married in their early twenties who stayed married and were still able to develop a strong sense of their own identity. But they are the exceptions. A recent study has shown the younger you are when you marry, the greater the likelihood you'll wind up divorced. If the marriage breaks up and there are children, then it will be a long time before you can call your life your own again. (On the other hand, I sometimes think if I'd had kids, all those years I spent married would make more sense.)

When I was in college, there was tremendous pressure to marry. That eased up during the '70s and for much of the '80s, but I sense the pressure is on again. It has to have some impact on young people when they keep reading how difficult it is when you're older to find someone to marry. Reading about AIDS could also make you want to rush headlong into marital monogamy.

My advice to my niece and others of her generation would be to wait. Life is a land mine of risks. It is scary, but it is an illusion that a husband or wife can make it less so. Only *you* can do that.

Past Voices Confirm the Changes

I find it reassuring when people from my past turn up again. It makes me think of life as a kind of conveyor belt; if you wait long enough, everybody you ever knew will come around a second time. That's better than seeing life as a parade and all those folks as just passing by.

The people who have popped up lately—by some quirk of fate, there has been a disproportionate number of them—happen to have more in common than just knowing me. They are all single, and they are going about their lives in a way that wouldn't have been possible for a single person the last time our paths crossed.

When Anna and I worked together in the '70s, for instance, if she'd had a child without benefit of a husband, she would not have sent out announcements. (Most likely, she wouldn't have had one at all; that was the decade when single professional women didn't seriously consider alternatives to abortion.)

I haven't seen Anna since her going-away party, so I was a little surprised to receive a powder-blue birth announcement from her, with all the information about the baby except the name of the father. I can only assume if I was on her mailing list, it must have been a pretty long list. Far from hiding the news, she clearly wanted everyone to know.

I understand from mutual friends that Anna was discouraged about the prospect of marrying. When she found out she was pregnant (she says it was an accident; these friends aren't so sure), she chose to have the baby and raise it alone. That must have been a difficult decision. I'm glad times have changed enough to allow her to have made it and to feel good about it. The baby present is in the mail.

I stepped further back into my past when I boarded a small plane in the mountains of New Zealand and heard a voice say, "Ruth-ie, is that you?" Nobody pronounces the "e" in my name except people who knew me in grammar school and people who don't know me at all.

As hard as it was for me to believe, of the sixteen passengers, one of them was Jeff N., who sat behind me in the fifth grade. (The story gets better. He had just come from visiting another classmate who is the reigning tai chi champion of Australia.) We did a lot of catching up during the fifty-minute flight. Jeff said he had been married briefly, but didn't really think marriage was for him. At some point I realized the woman beside him was his traveling companion. She was also his girlfriend.

It is no big deal anymore for unmarried couples to travel together. If no motel clerk in New Zealand cared that Jeff and his lady friend have different last names, you can be sure nobody in New York would care. But that wasn't true when Jeff and I were growing up in the '50s and early '60s—a time when single women wore "gold" wedding bands from the dime store when they checked in with a man and were terrified that, after registering as Mrs. So-and-So, they would fail to respond to that name. How much better it is now that this kind of ruse is no longer necessary and singles can explore the world with anyone they feel like.

When I got back from vacation, a sorority sister I hadn't heard from in twenty years called. Patsy was in San Francisco on business and had seen my byline in the paper. I had dinner with her and a man she introduced as her "spousal equivalent." They had been together for twelve years and couldn't find any compelling reason to marry. He already had children, and she had never wanted any. They led very independent lives; they didn't even live together. But they liked knowing the other was around for them.

Patsy and I laughed about the pressure to get married when we were in college—which, unlike me, she had resisted. The candlelight ceremony at our sorority house—in which we would solemnly gather in a circle and pass a candle until one girl blew it out, thereby announcing her engagement—was more the culmination of our education than a degree. Patsy's family and friends had stopped asking long ago when she was going to marry. It is enough, she said, that she is happy.

These voices from my past have a reassuring message for singles: In terms of options, we've never had it so good.